CRITICAL
VOICES

General Editor: David Jonathan Y. Bayot

DEREK ATTRIDGE
IN CONVERSATION

DEREK ATTRIDGE
IN CONVERSATION

DEREK ATTRIDGE

with

David Jonathan Y. Bayot and Francisco Roman Guevara

sussex
ACADEMIC
PRESS
Brighton • Chicago • Toronto

2 4 6 8 10 9 7 5 3 1

Published and distributed in the Philippines under ISBN 978-971-555-612-5 *by*
De La Salle University Publishing House
2401 Taft Avenue, Manila, Philippines 1004

This edition published and distributed in Great Britain in 2015 by
SUSSEX ACADEMIC PRESS
PO Box 139, Eastbourne BN24 9BP

and in the United States of America by
SUSSEX ACADEMIC PRESS
Independent Publishers Group
814 N. Franklin Street, Chicago, IL 60610

and in Canada by
SUSSEX ACADEMIC PRESS (CANADA)

Cover Design: John David Roasa.

British Library Cataloguing in Publication Data
A CIP catalogue record for this book is available from the British Library.

Library of Congress Cataloging-in-Publication Data
Attridge, Derek
Derek Attridge in conversation / Derek Attridge with David Jonathan Y. Bayot and Francisco Roman Guevara. — [Manila] :
De La Salle University Publishing House, 2015.
2015 100 pages ; 15 cm. — (Critical Voices)
ISBN: 978-1-84519-753-7 (pbk), in the Critical Voices series
1. Attridge, Derek—Criticism and interpretation. 2. Literature—History and ciriticism. I. Bayot, David Jonathan Y. II. Guevara, Francisco Roman. III. Title. IV. Series: Critical voices
PR9550.9.A87Z4 2015

Typeset & designed by Sussex Academic Press, Brighton & Eastbourne.
Printed by TJ International, Padstow, Cornwall.

DEREK ATTRIDGE
IN CONVERSATION

DAVID JONATHAN BAYOT: *Allow me to begin this conversational journey with you via* Peculiar Language. *Would it be accurate to say that it was your authorial intention for* Peculiar Language *to be a polemical response to the prevalent ethos and imperative during the eighties that "the birth of Theory must be at the expense of the death of literature" (to borrow the cadence of Roland Barthes's famous last line in "The Death of the Author")? And would you say that it is meant to "correct" a pervasive tendency within the academic community to misrepresent deconstruction, specifically the ideas of Jacques Derrida on writing, as a "coercive" critical gesture of anti-literature? I believe that your elucidation on the intellectual and institutional context of the book will enlighten the readers on the book's significance.*

DEREK ATTRIDGE: First, let me thank both of you for initiating this conversation, which I know will be revealing for me. Whether it will be revealing for anyone else, I'm not so sure, but I'll leave you to be the judges of that.

Now for your question. To be honest, the original impetus for *Peculiar Language* had little to do with any attempt to correct or modify an anti-literary bias in theoretical studies, something that wasn't very evident—or at least not very evident to me—when I began working on the question of the distinctiveness of literary discourse. The germ of my book was my reading of George Puttenham's 1589 treatise on poetry, *The Arte of English Poesie*, which I examined as part of my Cambridge PhD thesis around 1970. The thesis was on the Elizabethan experiments in quantitative meter, modeled on Latin and Greek versification—it later became my first book, *Well-Weighed Syllables* (1974)—but Puttenham's evident problems in identifying what could be said to constitute "poetry" seemed to me to invite further exploration. The opportunity came when, in 1984, I was invited to give a talk at the University of Toronto on a Renaissance topic. I was, at the time, in the USA on an exchange program for staff and students between my university, Southampton, and Rutgers, and the invitation came from someone I had met at one of our "Theory and Text" conferences (which I'll talk about later), Julian Patrick.

In the meantime, I had become interested in the wave of theoretical writing on literature emanating from France. Although

I had read Derrida, Lacan, and others while writing my PhD thesis, my main theoretical interest at that time had been in stylistics: the Russian Formalists, the Prague Structuralists, the work of Roman Jakobson, the Continental project of semiotic analysis, the American applications of Chomskyan linguistics to literary studies, and so on. In the early 1970s, Jonathan Culler, then a friend at Cambridge, lent me his recently completed Oxford DPhil thesis, which later became the immensely influential book *Structuralist Poetics* (published in 1975), and my second book—*The Rhythms of English Poetry*—was in part an attempt to provide an account of metrical and rhythmic "competence" in Chomsky's and Culler's sense, the mental habits and expectations that made it possible for speakers of English with some familiarity with the traditions of verse to respond to poetry in regular meters. Then, in the early 1980s, while teaching at the University of Southampton, I was fortunate in gaining two new colleagues who were fully engaged with French theoretical developments, Robert Young and Maud Ellmann. I remember reading the typescript of Robert's anthology *Untying the Text* while on sabbatical in France (where I was attempting to improve my French), along with a small library of French theoretical texts. (A little later, Isobel Armstrong was appointed as professor, an appointment that strengthened the theoretically disposed side of the department enormously: for the first time, we had someone in a senior position who sympathized with our attempt to introduce new kinds of work into the syllabus and into our research. It was a time of intense battles for the direction of the department, battles that were later to be replicated in other English departments in the country.) I now had a means of expression for my sense that the modes of literary criticism I had been taught, whether in South Africa or the UK, failed to do justice to the extraordinary power and inexhaustible richness of literature: it could be articulated in the language of undecidability, of *différance*, of the remainder, and so on.

Very little of what I was reading at this time could be described as "anti-literature"; literature in fact was of central importance to Barthes, Derrida, Kristeva, Lacan, Hélène Cixous, Paul de Man, Hillis Miller, Michael Riffaterre, Barbara Johnson, and most of the others I was reading. (Two other thinkers who became important to me later, and for whom literature was an important category, were Adorno and

Blanchot.) Even Foucault, whose work was to prove a potent resource for those wishing to dissolve the literary within a wider cultural field, clearly valued works of literature by, for instance, Roussel, Sade, and Artaud. But the question of the distinctiveness of literary language, or literary practice, or literary discourse seemed to me to be one that, in spite of the efforts of Jakobson, Mukařosvký, and others in one tradition and Derrida, Barthes, and their associates in another, remained unresolved. That invitation in 1984 to speak on Renaissance literature was a chance to investigate further one particular historical context for the question.

I found that the key term for Puttenham was *decorum*: when all the rules and specifications for literature had been observed, there remained a quality that could not, by definition, be defined, although it was this quality that made the crucial difference between a successful and an unsuccessful work. I realized that the structural relation between decorum and all the other features of the literary described by Puttenham was exactly what Derrida, in his reading of Rousseau, had termed *supplementarity*, the supplement being an addition that is at once outside and inside that to which it is added, like the supplementary volume to a set of dictionaries that adds further definitions to something already complete while at the same time testifying to, and making good, a crucial absence in the existing volumes. Having written that essay, I went on to explore other attempts to define the literary and found the same pattern again and again throughout the history of literary culture—in Aristotle, in Pope, in Wordsworth, in Saussure, in Jakobson. Always at a certain point in the account of the distinctiveness of literary language, there was an appeal to an extra indefinable quality, both outside the specifiable rules and conventions and yet absolutely essential to what made the text literary.

By 1984, I had also started teaching Joyce—a year-long course on *Finnegans Wake*, which I had first read as a graduate student and which I remained fascinated by, and thanks to Maud Ellmann, I had been introduced to a group of French Joyceans (mostly students of Hélène Cixous) who were bringing to Joyce studies the insights of French theoretical developments. I had been invited to join a panel at the 1982 centennial Joyce symposium in Dublin along with Maud,

Robert Young, Jean-Michel Rabaté, Daniel Ferrer, Colin MacCabe (later to be a colleague of mine at Strathclyde University), and others. And I had started publishing essays on Joyce and coediting with Ferrer a collection of recent French essays in English translation, published as *Post-Structuralist Joyce* in 1984. (The title was imposed on us by Cambridge, eager to cash in on a new trend—a choice that Derrida, whose essay on *Finnegans Wake* we included, termed *un peu marketing*.) We intended the volume to outrage the Joyce establishment and fully expected excommunication by the higher powers; instead, somewhat to our surprise, it became the vanguard of a movement that soon swept through Joyce studies.

My interest in Joyce was, again, in the transformation of the norms of language into something distinctive yet indicative of the normal operations of language and literature. I hadn't intended to write a book, but I realized that my essays on Joyce would make an appropriate second half of a study of the distinctiveness of literary language that could start with my work on earlier periods. I finished the book in, I think, 1986, the final pieces to be added being the introduction and a chapter bridging the gap between the Renaissance and the modern period, an essay whose major focus was Wordsworth's Preface to *Lyrical Ballads*, where the same undecidability was visible between, on the one hand, a desire to use "the real language of men" and, on the other, the necessity of being selective in that use—a selectivity that operated according a principle very like Puttenham's "decorum." Although I was more aware by then of the growth of cultural studies and of a move to displace literature from the center of attention, I still felt that an interest in what had constituted the literary and the continuation of that question into the present needed no justification. And I'm not sure that it does today—the idea that "Theory" was the brainchild of thinkers for whom literature was unimportant is an idea that has been promulgated more by its opponents than by its practitioners and has permeated media popularizations and perhaps undergraduate classrooms as a result. I've already given a list of names that prove the opposite: almost all those who played a major part in the theoretical wave of the last quarter of the twentieth century gave literature a prominent place in their thought.

Foucault, as I've mentioned, inspired a body of work in which the boundaries of the literary are dissolved, and there were some American and British theorists who borrowed concepts from Derrida or Deleuze or one of the other major continental philosophers in order to pursue a version of cultural studies that had no interest in literature, but this work never dominated the activity we call, for want of a better name, "Theory." The Marxist tradition provided another theoretical framework within which, for some critics at least, literature could be reduced to its role within a political and socioeconomic structure (often in opposition to what Marxist critics characterized as the "apolitical" character of "Theory"). Very late in the writing of *Peculiar Language*, I discovered the work of Pierre Bourdieu and in particular his book *Distinction* (which had been translated into English a couple of years before), and I'm sorry I didn't discover it earlier: I could have written a chapter on his sociological account of the literary, once again showing how such an account, important and insightful though it is, fails to provide a wholly exhaustive analysis and in its very failure reveals what is actually crucial to the distinctiveness of literature as a cultural practice. So, as it turned out, Bourdieu only features in the Introduction. I was and am in full agreement with accounts of literature as a social practice and institution, provided they are as subtle and informed as Bourdieu's, but my interest has always been in the ways in which some literary artists and literary works resist or problematize the conditions and conventions within which they are constituted.

So, to get back to your question: no, *Peculiar Language* didn't come about as a response to a perceived bias against literature but rather as a fascination with the ways in which literary difference has been articulated down the centuries. Your second question comes closer to the truth: I was aware that Derrida's writings had been subjected to a number of misreadings and distortions, including the idea that he was anti-literature, and I hoped that my illustration of the productivity of his thinking, especially of his elaboration of supplementarity, in understanding the workings of the literary field would do some good in setting the record straight. My readings of Joyce, also written in the early 1980s, were strongly influenced by Derrida, and it was at a Joyce symposium in Frankfurt in 1984 that I put to Derrida the idea of a collection of his essays on literature—but we'll come to that. (It was also thanks to Maud Ellmann that I found myself in a panel with Derrida at that symposium, with significant consequences for my intellectual career: she had to withdraw her participation and proposed me as a replacement.)

BAYOT: *How similar or different do you envision your representation of deconstruction to be compared to that of, say, Christopher Norris's* Deconstruction *(1982) or Jonathan Culler's* On Deconstruction *(1983) or* Deconstruction and Criticism *edited by Harold Bloom (1979)? Is the difference merely a matter of focus: theirs, for instance, on the theory of deconstruction and yours on the practical value of deconstruction to reading literary texts? Or is the difference more than just that reductive binary of theory and practice?*

ATTRIDGE: You've lumped together three rather different books in your question, and my answer has to be different in each case.

I recall reading Christopher Norris's *Deconstruction* with a certain amount of dismay, as it conveyed a very different sense of deconstruction from the one I had gained. The subtitle alone—*Theory and Practice*—gave me pause: if one had learned anything from reading Derrida, it was that deconstruction is not a method and does not provide a set of tools that can be applied to texts. And this is because the simple binary of "theory" and "practice" is in need of deconstruction—or, more accurately, necessarily deconstructs itself in any attempt to make the separation total. (This answers your last question, I guess: even if I did think of myself as being on the side of "practice" while the books you mention are on the side of "theory," the distinction is not one that can be sustained or that I would have been happy with.)

Of course, treating deconstruction as a method to be applied is precisely what a large number of critics, eager to be part of the new trend, did in the 1980s; what I hoped I was doing was not applying deconstruction but absorbing from my reading of Derrida a certain way of thinking, a certain understanding of the operation of signs, meanings, and power, and letting this influence my engagement with texts. In finding, for instance, that Wordsworth's account of a poetry that employs "the real language of men" rests on an undecidability, I wasn't attempting to "apply" Derrida's arguments about supplementarity to a text; rather, my appreciation of the structural logic of Wordsworth's attempt both to erase the difference between poetic and non-poetic language and at the same time to exclude certain kinds of expression was sharpened by my having read Derrida's *Of Grammatology*. My models were essays like Barbara Johnson's on Melville's *Billy Budd* and Cynthia Chase's on *Daniel Deronda*, which illuminate something central to the works they are analyzing that a familiarity with deconstruction had enabled them to perceive.

But to get back to Christopher Norris: I felt that in his 1982 book, and again in his 1987 volume *Derrida*, there was a valuable exposition of some of the key arguments in Derrida's work (as they existed up to the time of these books' publication) but that there was a fundamental lack of sympathy—resulting in a lack of understanding—with the most important and far-reaching aspects of Derrida's engagement with the philosophical tradition, aspects that can't be dissociated from the weight he attached to literature. Norris has increasingly sought to bring Derrida into the fold of philosophy as a practice governed by strict rules of logic, and while his insistence on this aspect of Derrida's thought has resulted in some important clarifications and is preferable to the opposite extreme of treating Derrida as a writer of wayward literary works, it leaves out of account much of what is most challenging about his relation to the tradition of Western philosophy. A more astute attempt to do something similar was Rodolphe Gasché's *The Tain of the Mirror*, published in 1986, a book I felt pushed against the grain of Derrida's thinking but was nevertheless immensely helpful in exposing the rigorous philosophical foundations of deconstruction. (A recent book that has similar virtues and limitations is Martin Hägglund's 2008 *Radical Atheism*.)

Jonathan Culler's *On Deconstruction* came closer to my own reading of Derrida and was a useful resource as I was writing *Peculiar Language*. Culler's clarity of exposition even when dealing with arguments that resist straightforward logic is admirable, and I've already mentioned the importance of *Structuralist Poetics* to me at an earlier stage of my career. Like me, Culler always has literature in mind when dealing with philosophical issues (whereas Norris, although he has a literary background, writes, in a sense, against literature). Indeed, Jonathan read the typescript of *Peculiar Language* for Cornell University Press and provided a positive endorsement for the cover of the paperback. You're right to imply that there's a fundamental difference between our two books: Culler took as his task the summarizing of examples of deconstruction, both in philosophical works and in deconstructive literary analyses, such as those of Johnson and Chase I've mentioned, whereas I was pursuing a particular thread through literary history with the aid of a deconstructive lens. And for both of us, given our desire to achieve as great a degree of clarity as is compatible with faithfulness to the thinkers whose work was our benchmark, the danger was and still is simplification and reductiveness. But I hope that the loss of some of the more perplexing attributes of deconstructive writing is a price worth paying for sharpness of focus and lucidity of exposition.

Deconstruction and Criticism is another matter altogether. For one thing, more than half of the book is taken up with important essays by Derrida and by Paul de Man (another significant influence on my early work on deconstruction, though I have always had a more vexed relationship with his thinking). They are manifestations of deconstruction being worked out in relation to literary texts, rather than the second-order engagement with it exemplified by Norris, Culler, and myself. (The original plan for the volume was that all the contributors would focus on Shelley's "Triumph of Life," but only de Man placed it at the center of his essay; Derrida's contribution was largely concerned with Blanchot's story *L'arrêt de mort* and included a brilliant discussion of translation in a running footnote.) Harold Bloom's contribution, largely a reading of John Ashbery's *Self-Portrait in a Convex Mirror*, is an example of his own theorizing of literary influence, and Geoffrey Hartman's piece, if I recall correctly, was an engagement with Wordsworth that dealt only briefly with deconstruction. The only essay that offered itself as an exposition of Derridean deconstruction was J. Hillis Miller's "The Critic as Host," a classic Millerian teasing out of the undecidable relation between host and parasite, including readings of a number of Shelley's poems. Miller, too, can be accused of a certain reductiveness in representing the work of Derrida and de Man in prose that sticks closer to the norms of discursive argumentation than does theirs, and again, I would say that the price is worth paying—as long as one continues to read Derrida and de Man as well as Miller.

BAYOT: *It's apparent—almost customary—in books on contemporary critical theory or post-structuralism to speak of Derridean deconstruction on the one hand and American (Yale) deconstruction on the other, with the latter perceived as a variant and/or deviant of the former in the course of the latter's re-iteration of the works of Derrida. Do you personally think that this is a tenable intellectual distinction?*

ATTRIDGE: Derrida met Paul de Man in 1966 at the famous conference on "The Languages of Criticism and the Sciences of Man" at Johns Hopkins University, and the two men discovered that they had many interests in common—most particularly that they were both fascinated by Rousseau's then-little-studied *Essay on the Origin of Languages*. De Man's criticism at that time had some similarities with Derrida's—this can be seen from his most important essays from the 1960s later published in *Blindness and Insight*—but it's clear that, for all the disagreements registered in his 1970 essay "Rhetoric of Blindness," de Man was profoundly influenced by his engagement at this time with Derrida's work. However, de Man's version of "deconstruction"—a term he was happy to adopt—was always significantly different from Derrida's (more different than Derrida was ever willing to admit, I think). So to this extent, it's possible to say that "Yale deconstruction" and "Parisian deconstruction" were distinguishable, for all their affinities, and that the former was more than a derivative version of the latter.

Also at the 1966 conference was J. Hillis Miller, the other Yale academic deeply influenced by Derrida. In Miller's case, the shift in critical approach was more dramatic: he had published a number of books in the 1960s influenced by the Geneva School, an offshoot of phenomenology, but after exposure to Derrida's work, he abandoned his earlier approach for a strongly Derridean understanding of literature. It is more legitimate in Miller's case to say that the deconstruction he promulgated was essentially a version of Derrida's, which is not to deny the considerable originality of his literary criticism but just to emphasize that all his work since 1970 has been inspired by Derrida's example and arguments. Sometimes, I feel that Miller adapts deconstruction in a manner that diminishes its radical character, though his willingness to grapple with the most difficult aspects of Derrida's work—always admitting when its difficulties become insuperable—is something I admire immensely. There are many places in Derrida's writing that I find I am baffled by, and it is reassuring to have others describe the same bafflement—especially someone as intelligent and widely read as Miller (and someone who was a close friend of Derrida).

As I suggested in talking about the volume *Deconstruction and Criticism*, the image it presents of a "school" of deconstructive critics based at Yale is misleading; the criticism of Geoffrey Hartman and Harold Bloom belongs to a different universe (or, rather, two different universes). De Man did have a number of students who went on to work in a deconstructive vein, often combining his approach with Derrida's.

Your question, I realize, is more about the possible existence of something we might call "American deconstruction" than about individual bodies of work, but I felt it was necessary to make some distinctions in order to answer properly. I think the range and variety of theory and criticism published in North America is so great that one can't responsibly speak of "American deconstruction" without qualification; much of this work is as rigorous and illuminating as Derrida's own. However, the late 1970s and 1980s did see the proliferation of a considerable amount of work that claimed allegiance to Derrida and deconstruction but was in fact a rather mechanical application of what were mistakenly taken to be the "methods" of the master's work. The relentless drive to be "up to date," the strong inheritance from the New Criticism, and the exotic appeal of Continental thought all played a part in this critical wave. Derrida himself referred to this body of writing as "deconstructionism" and saw it as a misunderstanding and misappropriation of his own work. There was a certain amount of such writing in other parts of the world, but there's no doubt that its primary location was the United States. It certainly didn't feature in France.

BAYOT: *You've just given us a wonderful account of the affiliations between "Parisian deconstruction" and "Yale deconstruction" and provided us with a useful map delineating the borders of each of these deconstructive territories. What I have found most revealing and intriguing is your statement that "it's possible to say that 'Yale deconstruction' and 'Parisian deconstruction' were distinguishable, for all their affinities, and that the former was more than a derivative version of the latter." Can you elucidate that statement further, especially the claim made by the last line about Yale deconstruction being more than a derivative version of Derridean deconstruction?*

ATTRIDGE: What I mean is that by the time he was exposed to Derrida's work, de Man had already evolved a powerful way of thinking about literary language, and although he was then influenced by Derrida, his work remained distinctive. It was more focused on literature, especially Romantic poetry and its inheritance, one of its major concerns being with the relations between symbol and allegory and between rhetoric and grammar. Hillis Miller, although he took de Man's work very seriously, was always closer to Derrida. I should also mention Shoshana Felman, who did extremely valuable work at Yale in a deconstructive mode, drawing on psychoanalysis to a greater extent than de Man or Miller. By "Yale deconstruction," then, I mean, for the most part, de Manian deconstruction, as evidenced in his work and that of those American scholars influenced by it, such as Miller, Barbara Johnson, Richard Rand, Andrzej Warminski, and Samuel Weber.

BAYOT: *Having said that about American deconstruction and its possible existence, would you say that there is such a thing as a British deconstruction represented by you, Geoffrey Bennington, or Christopher Norris, for example?*

ATTRIDGE: I don't believe that there is such a thing. Geoff Bennington's work springs from a profound sympathy with and understanding of Derrida's work, approached in the context of French cultural history and Continental philosophy, whereas, as I've indicated, Chris Norris's writing is influenced more by Anglo-

American philosophy, while my own interests are primarily literary. Robert Young and Maud Ellmann, too, have their own critical language—Robert moving in the direction of postcolonial studies, Maud drawing importantly on psychoanalysis. Some would argue that the distinctive quality of the British reception of Derrida lay in the stronger tradition of Marxist thought in this country, and while there is a certain amount of truth in this claim, none of those I've mentioned so far could be said to be centrally influenced by Marxism—though all, I suspect, would want to identify with socialism to some degree as a political program.

In the 1980s, there were some interesting clashes between those owing allegiance to Marxism and those who were influenced above all by deconstruction. The series of conferences we organized at Southampton under the title "Theory and Text," intended as a showcase for literary theory of a Continental cast, operated to some degree as counter-events to an already existing series of conferences at the University of Essex, called "The Sociology of Literature," which had a clear Marxist pedigree. Our conferences were perceived from the Essex perspective as insufficiently engaged with political demands and empirical realities; by contrast, we felt that the Essex conferences were hampered by a naive instrumentalism and untheorized attachment to "History." (I exaggerate somewhat, but the differences were certainly there.) Our second conference, on "Post-Structuralism and the Question of History," was designed specifically to counter the claim that we were uninterested in history and to demonstrate the sophistication of our understanding of historical processes and historical writing. The volume spawned by that conference is still in print after twenty-eight years, having sold over four thousand copies, so we must have gotten something right.

BAYOT: *You mentioned the presence of "untheorized attachment to 'history.'" What does that mean? How then should history be understood as a category or reality? What should be the proper degree of attachment of literary studies to history/historical studies and vice versa? In short, what is "history" for post-structuralism, and should it signify or be made "significant"?*

ATTRIDGE: These were the questions our conference and the subsequent volume were concerned with. Briefly, we were—and I am—suspicious of an appeal from literature to "history" that takes it to be an unquestionable and final limit, closing off questions of interpretation or evaluation, as if literature was the simple reflection of material reality. Of course, the best historians don't treat it in this way but understand that historical accounts remain interpretations and are always subject to revision, that history, in other words, as it comes to us in the present, is a text, in the broadest sense of this word (and so is the present). But there is sometimes a tendency in literary criticism to assume that the historian can provide the solid basis for interpretation and judgment that we literary readers cannot, a kind of cultural cringe that stems from the powerful authority claimed by— and often granted to—the empirical sciences. In a post-structuralist approach—again, speaking very broadly—history isn't given this privilege; a literary text is not merely the product or reflection of historical processes but is involved in those processes and often in a way that questions any straightforward conception of historical determination. My stress on singularity, invention, and otherness is one way of countering a too-simple notion of historical context: if the work of art brings into the cultural framework that which has been excluded, it interferes with the smooth unfolding of historical forces and can't be explained as simply a product of those forces. (A work of art that is nothing but such a product is unlikely to survive, except as an example for cultural historians.) The fullest critical study of the work in its historical context, then, is one that doesn't reduce the work to historical processes but one that explores the way in which the work resists as well as accords with those processes. And the critical study itself, situated as it is in a particular historical context, may be an uncomplicated reflection of that context—an expression of the cultural norms and habits of the time—or it may be an inventive engagement with both its own environment and that of the work of the past. You won't find it hard to discern which I prefer.

BAYOT: *Within the paradigm of deconstruction, is it still possible and sensible to speak of a "correct" reading of Derrida and for one to distinguish it from a "wrong" reading of the master? Or would you say that there are actually many Derridas or many phases of Derrida?*

ATTRIDGE: It's certainly possible to speak of *better* and *worse* readings of Derrida; I've already implied as much in describing, and regretting, the mechanical application of deconstructive "methods" to literary texts in the 1970s and 1980s. What Derrida, as early as *Of Grammatology*, called the "indispensable guardrail" of a reading that employs all the instruments of traditional criticism remains essential: there is no excuse for careless reading—and many readings of Derrida show carelessness (as do many translations of his work). Having said that, Derrida's own readings of many philosophers of the past show that it's possible to detect patterns of meaning that were not consciously placed there by the author but reflect broader structures and tensions in the intellectual and cultural context within which he or she was writing. A rich text, whether philosophical or literary, will yield more than one interpretation, depending on what thread is traced through it, what aspect of the language is attended to, and so on. So, there could be no "correct" reading of one of Derrida's texts if by this one means the only possible reading, though there are many—in fact an infinite number—of poor readings.

We could take an example I touched on earlier: Martin Hägglund's reading of Derrida's oeuvre in his brilliant book *Radical Atheism*. Hägglund takes as the key to Derrida's thinking his insight into the inseparability of space and time—the spacing of time and the temporalization of space—and builds on this a powerful argument about our investment in temporal living, with its potential for bad things to happen as well as good (even when we *think* our desire is for an atemporal state). Much of his book is taken up with a rebuttal of many of the most influential readings of Derrida, including those that take his work to constitute a major contribution to theology, to politics, and to ethics. My own sense is that Hägglund has very valuably identified an important strand in Derrida's thought and offered a useful corrective to some readings that have overlooked the strong conceptual basis for much of Derrida's work, but at the same time, he himself has given short shrift to some equally important strands in that work. (He and I had an interesting debate along these lines, a podcast of which can be seen on the Oxford University website and a version of which was published in the journal *Derrida Today*.) Any final judgment as to whether Hägglund is right and this or that critic of his arguments is wrong or vice versa is unlikely; the reason for this is that Derrida's work is far too complex for any single interpretation to exhaust it completely. There are, as you put it, many Derridas—all in one text. The conversation will continue, and no doubt some interpretations will be invalidated by common consensus, but new ones will continually arise and be assessed.

Another way of approaching this question is by way of what we can call "necessary infidelity": an interpretation of a complex text needs to do more than simply repeat it, if it is to be of any value, but in *not* repeating it, the interpreter is necessarily contributing something of his or her own. To be faithful to the singularity and inventiveness of the work being responded to means being unfaithful or at least writing in such a way that the opposition between fidelity and infidelity is problematized. One reason for this necessary infidelity is the coexistence of different strands in a rich philosophical text—for instance, Derrida's resolute evacuation of ethics from his arguments (he is interested, he says, in the "non-ethical opening of ethics") and at the same time his repeated recourse to ethical judgments and recommendations. To be faithful to the former, as Hägglund is, is to be unfaithful to the latter, and to be faithful to the latter, as I've tried to be, is to be unfaithful to the former.

The issue of Derrida's "phases"—whether his work can be said to shift from early to late—is a vexed one, and again, there is no simple answer. There are strong continuities in his thinking from start to finish, but it's also clear that certain preoccupations came to the fore as he grew older. The Derrida of *Of Grammatology* or *Introduction to Husserl's "Origin of Geometry"* doesn't stress the ethical or political implications of his thinking in the way that *Rogues* or *Philosophy in a Time of Terror* do. I remember attending the lecture on "Force of Law" at the Cardozo Law School at which he asserted that justice was "undeconstructible" and the surprise with which this statement was greeted. We had assumed that justice, like every other concept Derrida had analyzed, was subject to deconstruction. Perhaps we ought to have paid fuller attention to the implications of his earlier work, as there was in fact nothing here that contradicted his earlier thinking; nevertheless, it marked for me, and for many others, a new emphasis in his thinking.

BAYOT: *How is one supposed to understand Derrida's category of the "undeconstructible" in the context of his philosophy of deconstruction? Is he saying that there're really matters or, better, categories that have a "truth" status beyond reasonable doubt (e.g., "reason" itself)?*

ATTRIDGE: Not quite a "truth" status, but a status that places such categories (I'll stick with this word, as there is no really adequate term) outside the realm of the deconstructible—i.e., the realm occupied both by the main traditions of Western philosophy and by what is called "common sense." Derrida discussed a number of such categories, including justice, hospitality, the gift, and forgiveness. (Reason doesn't feature in the list, as it is a prime candidate for deconstruction, being one of the foundations of Western philosophy and common sense; Derrida provided deconstructive accounts of reason in a number of places, including the lecture entitled "The Principle of Reason: The University in the Eyes of its Pupils.") All these terms have an ethical tinge, but they don't function, for Derrida, simply as ethical norms or even unattainable ideals; instead, he sees them as something like forces that underpin or inform our daily actions when we are being ethical. To be more precise, he distinguishes, for instance, between unconditional hospitality and conditional hospitality— the hospitality we are actually able to offer, hedged as it is with limitations on the guest—between unconditional forgiveness and conditional forgiveness, between the gift properly so called and the imperfect gifts we actually give and receive. Similarly, he distinguishes between undeconstructible justice on the one hand and the law on the other, the latter being the inevitably limited attempt to provide an institutional vehicle for justice. In every case, the second category renders the first category workable in the real world and at the same time limits and distorts it. The conditions of possibility, as Derrida liked to say, are also the conditions of impossibility: what makes it possible to be hospitable, giving, forgiving, just, and so on at all is also what makes it impossible to be wholly so.

One might propose a similar relationship between a category of pure invention, where the artist would bring into being an artifact completely unconstrained by existing norms and possibilities, and the limited kind invention that actually happens. If the first were to take place, no one would recognize it; it's only by virtue of its engagement with the limitations of the world it enters that it is able to be known. But I wouldn't want to push this argument very far.

BAYOT: *Would it be accurate to say that* Acts of Literature *(1992) is, to a great extent, a continuation or reinforcement of your apology for the literary in* Peculiar Language, *this time with supporting documents from the author(ity) of deconstruction himself? Still on this book, what were your key considerations in the choice of essays by Derrida for inclusion in the volume? I'm wondering why certain essays that the readers would normally consider as Derrida's key discursive pieces on literature as writing are not included. I'm thinking, for instance, of "Signature Event Context."*

ATTRIDGE: There was certainly a personal and intellectual continuity between my work on *Peculiar Language* and my wish to collect some of Derrida's essays on literature in an anthology. During the 1980s, I had grown frustrated with the way Derrida's essays on philosophers and linguistic theorists were being used by literary critics to discuss literary texts, with the result that literature was being treated as if it were only the presentation of philosophical ideas, while his essays on literary texts were largely ignored. There was a reason for this, of course: the popular idea that "deconstructing a text" involved tracing in it an opposition and then overturning it—which was a crude version of Derrida's practice in his writing on figures like Saussure, Rousseau, Hegel, and Lévi-Strauss—provided a simple tool for literary analysis, whereas his writings on literary works displayed no such pattern of interpretation. The literary works Derrida was interested in were those that test the limits of language and thought, much as he did himself, and his response to every work he examined was different. This approach was congenial to me and in accord with my argument in *Peculiar Language* about literature's resistance to exhaustive analysis.

This is not to say that I found Derrida's literary analyses easy reading; in many ways, they tend to be more challenging than his discussions of philosophical texts. You feel Derrida is trying to work *with* the literary text, to elicit, bring forth, and develop its own most radical interventions in the intellectual, ethical, and cultural spheres, rather than exposing its hidden structures and contradictions.

Acts of Literature—a title I proposed to Derrida for this collection—was intended, therefore, to bring more fully to the attention of literary readers in the English-speaking world the importance of his responses to literary works. It's interesting that you should bring up "Signature Event Context," as I was very tempted to include it as the first essay in the collection. It's an essay that seemed—and still seems—to me an excellent starting point for understanding Derrida's arguments about the sign, meaning, context, and many other central issues. I hesitated, however, as it's not a reading of a literary work, so it would have been a borderline choice in terms of the book's rationale—and then I found out that Peggy Kamuf, who was putting together her own anthology of Derrida's writing at the time, was going to include it in its totality. Peggy and I discussed our respective selections to make sure there wasn't too much overlap between the two collections. So, as a way into Derrida's characteristic deconstructive procedures, I used instead Derrida's discussion in *Of Grammatology* of the "supplement" as it occurs in Rousseau's writing. This was also something of a borderline choice—is the *Confessions* a literary text?—but I decided that it was worth having because of the clear exposition of the structure of supplementarity, so central to Derrida's thinking on a host of topics, and the brilliant reading of a single word.

FRANCISCO ROMAN GUEVARA: *In your essay "Following Derrida," which is from your book* Reading and Responsibility: Deconstruction's Traces *(2011), you negotiate the achronological logic of Derrida by speaking about the inventiveness of his practice. I see this study of Derrida as a development of your scholarly investment in prosody, particularly rhythm. Can you elaborate further on the rhythms of Derrida and the necessity of studying his rhythms to the revaluation of his oeuvre?*

ATTRIDGE: I wrote "Following Derrida" in 2003 as the result of an invitation to contribute to an issue of the French series *Cahiers de l'Herne* on Derrida's work; it was translated into French by Christine Roulston for the volume. I hadn't thought of this piece as related to my writing on prosody (but this is to raise the whole question of the relation between the different fields in which I have worked, a question that I don't think I am necessarily the best person to answer). To speak of Derrida's rhythms is to use the word in a semi-metaphorical way; that's to say, it's largely the rhythms of his thinking one is interested in, rather than the rhythms of his sentences. True, we could analyze the rhythms of his French prose, especially his rather extraordinary handling of syntax, and this might illuminate some of the ways in which his mind worked, but it would be a very tricky task. A study of his thought in various texts as a rhythmic matter would also be difficult but could be very rewarding. Why is it he starts so often with a phrase or a sentence whose ambiguities form the originating impulse of the lecture or essay? (I deliberately mimicked this procedure in starting my piece with the statement "Derrida is hard to follow," following his practice as I raised the question of "following," in the senses of coming after, chasing, and trying to understand.) What are we to make of the long sections that sometimes occur in parentheses? Why do some of his most brilliant insights come in footnotes? (I think of the note on *mimesis* in "The Double Session" and the long notes at the end of "Passions"—the latter is a place where one of his most illuminating discussions of the nature of the "literary" occurs.) The publication of the seminars is giving us an insight into the rhythm of these sessions, somewhat similar to the long lectures he gave later in his life: a style of exposition that works by gradual accretion of examples and ideas, rather than the more concise style of his earlier published work.

As he himself would have insisted, the rhythms of his speaking and writing can't be dissociated from the arguments he is making. This might be thought of as another respect in which his work partakes of the "literary," though the same would be true of any philosopher or literary critic. Some philosophical texts try to excise this dimension and to come as close to mathematical logic as possible, but this too is a stylistic decision that produces a distinctive rhythm, suggestive of a certain mode of thought. Others—including some of Derrida's texts— operate on the borderline between literature and philosophy.

GUEVARA: *In the same essay, you briefly negotiate the productive ambiguities in the English translations of Derrida together with how it unfolds in the original French:*

Take the work I have read most recently: "L'animal que donc je suis" in L'animal autobiographique. *(How will the title of this essay be translated into English? "Je suis" can be "I am"—a reading strengthened by the echo of Descartes' cogito in French—and "I follow." Anyone who knows the essay will know that I have been following Derrida in taking advantage of the ambiguities of the verb "to follow," even though these ambiguities work differently in French and in English.)*

At the same time, in chapter 4 of Peculiar Language, *titled "Language as History/History as Language: Saussure and the Romance of Etymology," you mention Derrida arguing for the etymological relation between "hymen" and "hymn" as an act of "...turning the etymological dictionary against itself, using the power of etymology to undermine the easy mastery of language implied in much of our literary and philosophical tradition and to shake our assurance in fixed and immediately knowable meanings" (PL, 123). Similar to translation, these engagements with etymology seem to adhere to the necessity of shaking one's assurance in "fixed and immediately knowable meanings," which is a significant gesture in Derrida's practice. Gayatri Chakravorty Spivak talks about the difficulty of translating Derrida's* Of Grammatology *(1976) in the corrected edition by citing Derrida's ideas about translation from* Positions *(1981):*

> *Within the limits of its possibility, or its* apparent *possibility, translation practices the difference between signified and signifier. But, if this difference is never pure, translation is even less so, and a notion of* transformation *must be substituted for the notion of translation: a regulated transformation of one language by another, of one text by another. We shall not have and never have had to deal with some "transfer" of pure signifieds that the signifying instrument—or "vehicle"— would leave virgin and intact, from one language to another, or within one and the same language.*

Can you talk further about the rhythmic experiences of following Derrida's writing in English and French, especially in the work you feel the most indebted to in your writing of The Singularity of Literature *(i.e., those you mention in the appendix like those works from* Acts of Literature, The Gift of Death, Altérités, *"Afterword," "Force of Law," "Che cos'è la poesia?," "Passions,"* Aporias, Specters of Marx, *"La littérature au secret," and/or "A Self-Unsealing Poetic Text")? And can you talk about how this constant transformation has informed your insistence on following Derrida over the past thirty or so years?*

ATTRIDGE: There are a number of French scholars of Derrida who are equally at home in English as in their native language (I've already mentioned Jean-Michel Rabaté in the context of Joyce studies; his friendship and intellectual example has been just as important for me in the context of Derrida studies). There are also a number of English-speaking British and American scholars of Derrida who are equally at home in French (to name a few, Peggy Kamuf, Rachel Bowlby, Geoff Bennington, Barbara Johnson, Michael Naas, Thomas Dutoit). I have never been intimate enough with the French language to engage with Derrida's writing in the way that such scholars have; I need to work with a dictionary at my elbow. So my major engagement with Derrida has been with English translations, and I am profoundly grateful for the work of so many excellent translators.

When I set out to bring together translations of Derrida's texts on literary works in what became *Acts of Literature,* I assumed that my task would be to reprint the translations and provide some introductory commentary and notes. However, in re-reading the pieces I wanted to include, I found myself from time to time coming across sentences that seemed not quite right, and when this started happening rather frequently, I decided to check against the French original, hoping that my knowledge of the language (and use of the dictionary) would enable me to assess whether there was a fault in the translation. It turned out that there often *was* a mistranslation (though I must say immediately that this wasn't the case with any of the translators I have just named). I found this process of testing the translation against the original absorbing and illuminating; it was also testimony to the precision of Derrida's writing, since the obscurities in the English often turned out not to be there in the French. (Much could be said about the consequences of Derrida's having been read through the medium of translations—and not always the most accurate translations—in the English-speaking world.) Often, of course, it wasn't so much a question of obscurity as one of multiple meanings that simply couldn't be transferred into English. Gayatri Spivak's comment highlights the fact that in any translation, there is transformation, and all the more so when the original plays with polysemy, sound effects, and etymological sedimentations.

So, the texts you mention, all of which have been important to me, have been effective for me mostly through translation. I should mention one exception, since it was a crucial moment in the development of my interest in Derrida's work: in 1982, I attended a lecture he gave at the Royal Philosophical Society in London. At that time, he was reluctant to speak in English and gave the lecture in French; somewhat to my surprise, I found I was able to follow the argument quite well, and the whole experience—this was the first time I had seen and heard Derrida in the flesh—was enormously exciting. The lecture was entitled "Devant la loi," and it became, and has remained, one of my favorite texts by Derrida. I included it in *Acts of Literature* under its English title (echoing, of course, the fable by Kafka that it offers a dazzling reading of), "Before the Law."

When I came to write *The Singularity of Literature*, I had read a great deal of Derrida's work and that of commentators on Derrida, as well as a host of other philosophy and literary theory, but I wanted to write a book that didn't assume knowledge of this work and that didn't constantly relate its own arguments to that of others. Although I was heavily indebted to the reading I had done, I kept most of the references to it in an appendix on "Debts and Directions," so that it could serve as a guide for further reading as well. This approach didn't go down very well with commissioning editors: the manuscript was rejected by several publishers (relying in some cases on remarkably obtuse reader's reports) before an admirable editor named Liz Thompson at Routledge read it and quickly put it into production. I'm now working on a sequel that will attempt to answer some of the further questions raised by the book and further elaborate some of the points I sketched rather briefly in the interests of concision.

BAYOT: *As early as 1974, your book* Well-Weighed Syllables *already indicated your scholarly fascination with language in terms of its materiality. Two more books, at least, demonstrated the persistence of your passion for the "linguistics of writing" (as one of the volumes you coedited names it):* The Rhythms of English Poetry *(1982) and* Poetic Rhythm: An Introduction *(1995). May we know the personal and academic context for such scholarly interest?*

ATTRIDGE: It's hard to say what the origins of this interest were. Perhaps growing up in a multilingual culture had something to do with it: my family and the community to which we belonged—in Pietermaritzburg, South Africa—all spoke English, but the majority of the population of the city spoke isiZulu, a language with a very different repertoire of speech sounds, including a number of clicks (which still come naturally to me but which I find my friends in this country and the USA struggle to pronounce). My early education was in a dual-medium school, that is to say there were classes taught through the medium of Afrikaans as well as in English, and throughout my high school career, I was taught Afrikaans, including Afrikaans poetry. (This was my least favorite part of the school curriculum, largely for political reasons—Afrikaans was associated with the apartheid government—but I am returning to the language in some of my current work.) I also took Latin as a school subject and enjoyed the practice of scansion, whereby lines of verse could be shown to have a clear structure, determinable if you knew the rules. An early love of poetry and a system of education in which learning poems by heart and reciting them in the classroom was normal may have contributed. I enjoyed acting (my first part on the high school stage was as a Scottish peasant woman—I'm sure my accent was atrocious!) and participating in the debating society. Then, four years of classes in a university English department (at the University of Natal in my hometown) dedicated to close reading or "Practical Criticism" no doubt played its part; I also studied German for my undergraduate degree and enjoyed German poetry. I wrote poetry occasionally, though I found what I was best at was writing pastiches of other poets. And I was active in the university's dramatic society, which I believe still holds a silver cup with my name engraved on it for having given the best dramatic performance of the year in a play by Harold Pinter.

The detailed readings of poetry I was expected to produce at the University of Natal included comments on sound and rhythm, and— through some personal predilection I'm not capable of analyzing—I found this aspect of the task particularly congenial. I wrote my undergraduate dissertation on the poetry of Emily Dickinson (in 1963, her work was not nearly as well-known as it became in later years) and relished her use of the four-beat hymn measure. I also discovered classical music at university and was fascinated by the role of temporal structure in symphonic form: the creation of tension and release by various means—harmony, rhythm, melody, timbre, volume—seemed to me something that happened, with some of the same means and some different, in verse, though the necessary analytic tools were not available.

When I left South Africa to take up a scholarship at Cambridge (I had a two-year scholarship, so I enrolled as an "affiliated student" to take a second bachelor's degree), I found that English studies was a much wider and more varied field than I had been led to believe at Natal: historical, biographical, psychological, and other approaches flourished alongside the close reading I had been taught. As I've mentioned, I learned French (for some reason, German wasn't available as part of the English Tripos, which annoyed me at the time, although in retrospect, I was grateful for being forced to pick up another language). When I had to devise a topic for a PhD—I had been lucky enough to be awarded a scholarship by the university—I chose Elizabethan love poetry. My aim was to compare Renaissance theories of love, such as the Neoplatonic philosophy of Marsilio Ficino, with the practice of Elizabethan poets. The first task was to read carefully all the sixteenth-century treatises on poetry in English. When I did this, I found the most puzzling feature to be the pages and pages devoted to the question of domesticating Latin meters in English. I wanted to get this aspect of the treatises out of the way as quickly as possible and thought all I needed to do was read whatever published studies there were so I could summarize their findings. Unfortunately, nothing I read seemed to do justice to the treatises or to the actual experiments undertaken by Elizabethan poets such as Sidney and Spenser in writing

English verse in classical meters. All right then, I told myself, I'll undertake the task myself; it can form part of the introduction of the thesis. Three years later, I found I had written an entire thesis on these quantitative experiments.

This work involved close engagement with the question of the sounds of poetry. The first question that had to be answered was, "How did the Elizabethans pronounce Latin?" That meant studying educational treatises in English and Latin and looking for clues wherever I could find them. (Some of the most useful clues came from writers trying to devise a new alphabet truer to actual pronunciation than the standard one: their examples were sometimes in Latin.) The next stage was examining the experimental poems in English to deduce what the poets thought they were doing and how the original readers might have read them. I guess by the time I'd finished this project, the question of the materiality of language and the role of sound in poetry were pretty well embedded in my brain.

While working on the Elizabethan materials, I had read a fair number of books and articles on English prosody more generally and found most of these unsatisfactory. When I'd finished *Well-Weighed Syllables*, I wanted to move to a broader treatment of rhythm in English poetry, and I was able to do this in the late 1970s once my teaching was under control. (I had taken up a position teaching Romantic literature at Southampton University in 1973, after two years as a research fellow at Oxford University.) The result was *The Rhythms of English Poetry*.

GUEVARA: *In a response to Richard Cureton's response to your review essay titled "Beyond Metrics: Richard Cureton's Rhythmic Phrasing in English Verse" (1996), you mentioned how your thoughts on rhythm and meter have changed since the publication of* The Rhythms of English Poetry *(1982). Can you discuss some of these changes and how they might be potentially present in your latest book,* Moving Words: Forms of English Poetry *(2013)? At the same time, can you talk about the reasons for the dearth of metrical and beat prosodic practices in late-twentieth-century poetic practice and the reasons behind the resurgence of these pattern orientations today?*

ATTRIDGE: I'm not sure my thoughts have changed that much, though I have suggested adjustments to the mechanics of scansion that I originally proposed in *The Rhythms of English Poetry*. If you put the date of that book—1982—next to my comments above, you'll see that when it came out, I was deeply involved in French literary theory and the writings of James Joyce. These new interests are reflected only a little in the book—at a late stage, I added some paragraphs in which I speculated on the operation of meter as a depersonalization of language—but by the time it appeared, my intellectual focus was no longer on the sounds and structures of poetry. I remember a review of *The Rhythms of English Poetry* in the *Times Educational Supplement* that began with an anecdote about the reviewer's conversation with his wife, who had asked him, "How could anyone write a whole book on *that*?" Another review—a much more positive one—was written for the *Times Literary Supplement* by the poet Tom Disch, who, when I contacted him, invited me to dinner in New York; I recall his surprised comment when he opened the door: "I thought you must be much older!" It was definitely time to turn to a sexier field of study! The book has lasted well, however, and thirty years on, it is still frequently quoted.

One immediate consequence of publishing *The Rhythms of English Poetry* was an invitation from Colin MacCabe, then Head of the Department of English Studies at the University of Strathclyde in Glasgow, to apply for a chair there. Colin, who was widely known as a result of the "MacCabe affair" at Cambridge involving a refusal of tenure, partly as a result of his commitment to French theory, had initiated a program at Strathclyde on literary linguistics and wanted me to strengthen this aspect of the department. But of course, we had a lot in common as regards our theoretical interests as well, and one of the first things we did together, with our younger colleagues Nigel Fabb and Alan Durant, was to mount a conference on "The Linguistics of Writing" to which we invited all the international stars we could think of. (So impressive was the advertised lineup that Terry Eagleton contacted me asking to be added to it; my colleagues were reluctant, but I persuaded them that he would be a valuable addition. I should have known better—he pulled out before the conference took place.)

The moment I treasure most was when I was able to introduce Jacques Derrida to Raymond Williams. The volume David mentioned in an earlier question emanated from this conference; there was also a slightly tongue-in-cheek TV program presented by David Lodge.

Going back to *The Rhythms of English Poetry*, I remained conscious that the book I had written, which I had intended to be a useful text for the classroom, had turned out to be too complex and academic to serve that function very well. After I had been at Rutgers University for a while—I moved there in 1988—and had published *Peculiar Language* and *Acts of Literature*, I decided to write a short introductory book on rhythm and meter in English poetry that would be more widely accessible. That was where I revised some of my thinking about scansion, though not my basic understanding of poetic rhythm as inhering in mental and physical habits acquired in both the learning of a particular language and the inculcation of simple rhythmic forms in childhood. However, I got carried away in exploring new dimensions of the subject, and *Poetic Rhythm: An Introduction* turned out not to be the book I had in mind: although simpler than the earlier study, it was still too advanced for the undergraduate or high school classroom. A few years later, I was contacted by Tom Carper, a poet and retired university professor, who had been successfully using a simplified version of my prosodic approach to teach the subject and was hoping to find a publisher for the little handbook he had produced. When he had no success in persuading publishers, we decided to revise the handbook, with some additional material by me, and offer it as a joint effort. The coauthored book was accepted by Routledge and published in 2003 as *Meter and Meaning: An Introduction to Rhythm in Poetry*, a text that is widely used in the classroom.

Moving Words, my most recent book, is a compilation of essays on poetry from the past thirty-four years; the earliest is a study of the use of rhymed couplets in tragic drama in English and French, published in 1979, and the most recent is a discussion of the poetic theories and practice of J. H. Prynne and Don Paterson. I was pleased to find that the 1979 essay, though it required considerable updating in the light of newer translations of Racine and further studies of the question of rhyme, still represented something I wanted to be read, and the same was true of essays written in the intervening years. So, I would want to emphasize continuity rather than change.

As for the reasons for the shift away from regular meters in the twentieth century and the (possible) return in more recent years, that would require a book in itself. The chapter of *Moving Words* in which I consider the evidence for a return of a critical interest in formal matters doesn't really deal with the question of poetry's trajectory over this period. British and Irish poetry, in any case, has always included a strong current of formal interest in meter and rhyme, from Auden and MacNeice to Larkin, Heaney, Hill, Muldoon, and Paterson.

GUEVARA: *In your introductory essay to* Acts of Literature *titled "Derrida and the Questioning of Literature," you talk about Derrida's conception of the literary text:*

> *For Derrida the literary text is not, therefore, a verbal icon or a hermetically sealed space; it is not the site of a rich plenitude of meaning but rather a kind of emptying-out of meaning that remains potently meaningful; it does not possess a core of uniqueness that survives mutability, but rather a repeatable singularity that depends on an openness to new contexts and therefore on its difference each time it is repeated.*

While Derrida makes a distinction between literature and poetry in your interview with him titled "This Strange Institution Called Literature," can you discuss the ways in which the aforementioned experience of the literary text and Derrida's concept of iterability is available in twenty-first-century English poetry in spite of today's embarrassment or aversion with reading metrical, phrasal, and rhythmic forms? This question is vaguely similar to my previous question about the rhythms of Derrida's writings precisely because I'm quite curious about the productive convergences between your scholarly engagements with Jacques Derrida and English prosody. I'm especially interested in the possibility of thinking about an ethics of prosody and what that might look like in the writing and reading of twenty-first-century English poetry.

ATTRIDGE: Derrida's account of the literary work, as I understand it, is relevant to any text that responds to a "literary" reading. That is to say, if you approach the text as if it were a literary work, if you engage with it as an event that has the potential to open up new horizons of meaning and feeling, an event that takes to the limit what language can do, and you find that this approach is fruitful, that the work does in fact do more than provide information or state moral injunctions, that the act of reading it is itself an event that exposes you to new possibilities of sense and emotion, *then* it is a literary work—at least for you at a particular time and place (and probably more widely for the culture that has produced your manner of thinking and feeling). Form, I would argue, plays a crucial role in this experience: it is because language is formed in a certain way—in terms of lexis, syntax, rhythm, layout on the page, sound patterns, structuring of themes, handling of plot, and so on—that it can happen as an event. Reading a text as literature involves being alert to these formal features, letting them have an effect as you proceed through the words.

I don't feel that any particular formal features have a greater or lesser potential as elements in this process. Regular meter and rhyme constitute one way in which form can work in poetry—they can be mimetic of sounds or movements in the word, they can highlight certain words and phrases, they can bring together for comparison or contrast words that otherwise would not be associated, and so on. But verse that lacks these formal features has others, if it works successfully as poetry. (The culture may at first have no way of dealing with them, however: new ventures in poetic form may take time to be appreciated, as readers develop the necessary reading strategies.) For instance, in *Poetic Rhythm*, I devoted a chapter to syntax, which is a potential formal resource in most kinds of poetry, whether or not it uses rhyme and meter.

As for an ethics of prosody, I'm not sure! I see the responsibility of both readers and writers as lying in an openness to the new, the different, the other; a willingness to be changed by this exposure. Formal features can be a way of registering otherness. Many poets have testified that having to conform to a predetermined set of constraints is actually a highly creative situation: searching for a rhyme or a phrase that will suit the meter may result in completely unsuspected kinds of meaning or varieties of emotion.

BAYOT: *At what point in your scholarly life did James Joyce become prominent as an object of knowledge quest? Would you say that your interest in Joyce—one of the most "language-centered" authors—is a development of/from the "linguistics of writing" that preoccupies your books on the words, the lines, the pronunciation, and the rhythm of English poetry?*

ATTRIDGE: My initial training in university English studies, in South Africa, was in a department dominated by the principles and exclusions laid down by F. R. Leavis, whose influence in the colonies and ex-colonies during the 1950s and 1960s was extraordinarily pervasive. One of Leavis's blind spots was Joyce: he rejected the Irish writer's work as superficial and mannered (influenced perhaps by his hero among contemporary writers, D. H. Lawrence, who couldn't stand Joyce). So, Joyce was absent from the syllabus, and it was not until I was on the Warwick Castle sailing from Cape Town to Southampton in 1966, on my way to Cambridge, that I read *Ulysses*. I found it an astonishing book, and I still treasure the Bodley Head edition, whatever its shortcomings as a text, for the pages of beautifully and spaciously laid out print that engrossed me on that twelve-day voyage from my home country into the unknown. I don't remember when I first read Joyce's earlier fiction, but I do remember that it was as a graduate student (working, as I've said, on Elizabethan poetry) that I tackled *Finnegans Wake*, reading it slowly from start to finish with a number of guides and glossaries by my side.

At this stage and for a long time afterwards, I had no thought of teaching Joyce (other than short passages in "Practical Criticism" classes), let alone of writing and publishing on his work. As I've said, it was a decision, many years later, to follow up my excitement and pleasure in reading *Finnegans Wake* by offering a year-long course at Southampton University that kick-started my academic interest. And this process was very much tied up with my discovery of the work of French philosophers and theorists. Joyce was, of course, very important to many of the theorists I was reading—Derrida, Kristeva, Lacan, and Cixous had all been influenced by Joyce.

And yes, the attraction of Joyce was very much connected with my enjoyment of poetry and of "language at full stretch," as Winifred Nowottny memorably put it. I must also confess to a fascination with literary works that challenge the reader, whether through their experiments with language or genre or through their huge scope. Pound's *Cantos*, Proust's *A la recherche,* Pynchon's and Nabokov's novels, Coetzee's fiction…At the moment, I'm writing a piece on two remarkable novels written in Afrikaans and ably translated into English, Marlene van Niekerk's *Triomf* and *Agaat*—both very long and extraordinarily creative in their handling of language. (I think something similar lies behind my admiration for and pleasure in Wagner's operas.)

BAYOT: *And at what point in the trajectory of your scholarship has Derrida become a critical figure? And how did that come about—was it a conference with or on Derrida? Or was it a book by/on Derrida? Was it Joyce? Or could it be that Derrida is simply the logical choice of a philosopher whom a critic should turn to if his interest in text/literature is on its materiality?*

ATTRIDGE: My first encounter with Derrida's work must have been when I found in the Cambridge English Faculty library Macksey and Donato's collection *The Language of Criticism and the Sciences of Man* (later retitled *The Structuralist Controversy*), the papers from the 1966 Johns Hopkins conference at which Derrida, then more or less unknown in the English-speaking world, gave the lecture "Structure, Sign and Play." The volume was published in 1970, and it would have been soon after publication that I read it, since I was finishing my PhD thesis at that time. But I recall that I didn't get much out of Derrida's essay; its mode of argument was foreign to me. About the same time, as I mentioned, Jonathan Culler lent me his Oxford DPhil thesis, in which there was some discussion of Derrida. And I must have heard about Derrida from Stephen Heath, who was, I think, a research fellow at the time and did some teaching for the colleges. In 1971, Stephen, together with Christopher Prendergast and Colin MacCabe (not known to me at that time), brought out a slim volume called *Signs of the Times: Introductory Readings in Semiotics*, which printed essays by, among others, Julia Kristeva and Philippe Sollers and included an interview with Roland Barthes. This cheaply produced book, printed in an almost unreadable typeface, was indeed a sign of the times, or the coming times at least, and included many references to Derrida's work, especially *De la grammatologie* and *L'écriture et la différence* (which of course had not been translated at that time). (I still have my rather worn copy.) So Derrida's name, at least, was very much in the air in the early 1970s.

Of Grammatology, translated by Gayatri Spivak, was finally published in 1976. I can't remember when I first read it, but it was probably a couple of years later. I've already told the story of the arrival of Robert Young and Maud Ellmann in the Southampton department; I participated in and was enthusiastic about the appointments, having read their work and some issues of the *Oxford Literary Review* that they were involved in, so I must have heard enough about post-structuralism to want to push the department in that direction through new hires.

It wasn't just Derrida who caught my attention, though; I enjoyed Roland Barthes's work very much, and I remember travelling to Oxford to hear Harold Bloom speak and being impressed by his articulate and punchy demolition of a number of sacred cows. The Foucault of "The Order of Discourse" and *Les Mots et les Choses* (rather oddly translated as *The Order of Things*) were also important to me. I certainly don't think that Derrida is the only philosopher to turn to if you're interested in the materiality of literary language, but it's true that he was the one I returned to again and again.

As I've said, I saw Derrida speak in London in 1982, but I didn't meet him until 1984, first at the French embassy in New York at the launch of my friend Richard Rand's translation of *Signéponge* (*Signsponge*) and later that year at the Frankfurt Joyce symposium. He had by then read some of my writing on Joyce, and it was at that symposium that he agreed to the project that became *Acts of Literature*. I was struck by his generosity and tact and by his willingness to take seriously the projects of a young and little-known academic.

BAYOT: *Putting Derrida and Joyce side by side in the context of your scholarship, one has the tendency to see Derrida's philosophy of language/writing as a critical "framework" you've discovered and appropriated to read Joyce in order do his work justice. Could it be that, in reality, it's the other way around: that it was actually Joyce and your devotion to his work through the years that enabled you to see the logic of Derrida's difficult discourse on language, writing, and literature? Or could it be that your parallel interest in Derrida and Joyce complement your understanding of both authors?*

ATTRIDGE: I suspect the last way of putting it is closest to the truth. My interest in Derrida and my interest in Joyce (and, in particular, in *Finnegans Wake*) were aroused and grew at the same time, and the two were mutually reinforcing. Derrida helped me understand the working of the *Wake*, and being absorbed in the *Wake* helped me get to grips with Derrida's writing. The first piece of writing I did on Joyce, in 1982, was clearly influenced by my engagement with Derrida (though it was on *Ulysses*, not the *Wake*), and the first piece I wrote on Derrida, in 1984, was for the Frankfurt Joyce symposium, for a panel on "Deconstructive Criticism of Joyce."

GUEVARA: *In your introduction to* Peculiar Language, *you talk about two linguistic theorists who are significant to the book:*

> *...Saussure and Jakobson, although largely in agreement on their general view of language, come down on opposite sides of this fence: for Saussure, apparent instances of motivation such as onomatopoeia are marginal phenomena, but for Jakobson they represent, in his phrase, "the essence of language." Joyce's texts contradict neither. It is the principle of arbitrariness, allowing infinite combinatory possibilities of form and content, which provides Joyce with his material and scope, while it is the principle of motivation, the never-fading desire*

on the part of the language-user to find or to make a system
of signs in which form and content indissolubly cohere, which
produces the energy and pleasure by which Joyce's texts, and
their readings, are propelled. (PL, 11)

To slightly dovetail on David's previous question, is it possible
to say that Derrida occupies the same position Joyce occupies in your
engagement with Saussure and Jakobson? Or is it possible that your
engagement with Derrida is a way of engaging contradicting principles
of thought? What or who are these principles or thinkers and what are
the circumstances and conditions in which Derrida contradicts neither
of them?

ATTRIDGE: A very interesting question. Yes, I think it would be
true to say that Derrida, like Joyce, occupies a position that is neither
that of Saussure nor that of Jakobson but partakes of both. Derrida's
reading of Saussure in *Of Grammatology*—like his reading of many
thinkers—does ample justice to the important advances the Swiss
linguist made to our understanding; he takes Saussure's insight
into the way a sign within a system has meaning only in relation to
other signs that could be present but aren't and develops this into
an argument about the *trace*, which is neither fully present nor fully
absent. But he also highlights Saussure's failure to escape what he
sees as the persistent assumption in Western thought that speech—
or rather hearing-oneself-speak—represents the essential nature of
language, whereas writing is regarded only an unreliable secondary
mode of communication, divorced from its originator and its
addressee. Derrida shows how this hierarchy is undermined within
Saussure's own discourse: speech is a use of language that has all the
properties that writing is condemned for. Joyce had no theoretical
understanding of these issues, but his work (especially *Finnegans
Wake*) gloriously capitalizes on the openness to new meanings that
language—whether spoken or written—can acquire in new contexts
and must acquire if it is to operate at all.

Then, in *Glas*, Derrida addresses Saussure's views on
onomatopoeia, views which are, not surprisingly, hostile, since
onomatopoeia contradicts the principle of the arbitrariness of the

linguistic sign. Derrida reveals that there is something at work in the relation between the sound of words or parts of words—he's especially interested in the sound made by the letters *gl*—that can't be fully accounted for in terms of arbitrary associations. Without reverting to a notion that the sounds of language are motivated (which is to say without adopting the Jakobsonian position that motivation represents the essence of language), he throws a spanner in the works by appealing to what I have called the desire of the language user that sounds *should* be motivated. Joyce, too, appeals constantly to that desire, complicating and enriching his exploitation of the arbitrariness of language by drawing on the associations within certain languages between particular sounds and particular categories of meaning— associations explored theoretically by Jakobson.

In my own thinking about onomatopoeia, I came to a conclusion that draws on the insights of both Saussure and Jakobson, in a way that doesn't exactly follow Derrida but could be said to be Derridean in its suspicion of both Jakobsonian essentialism and Saussurean arbitrariness. I revisited this issue in a recent piece on the relation of sound and sense in lyric poetry, which appears as a chapter of *Moving Words*.

BAYOT: *At this point, I must admit to you that I personally find Ray Monk's idea of philosophical biography very appealing: that one's knowledge of a thinker's life—the processes of his living/thinking— is crucial to the readers' understanding of the attitude and spirit animating the ideas of the thinker concerned. In fact, my wanting to possess more of that kind of knowledge is one of my principal motivations for starting the* Critics in Conversations *series. I'm interested in this "genre" of scholarship (if we can call it that) because I agree with Monk that it's important to understand what the philosopher or critic thought he or she was doing in this or that project. Such an understanding, I believe, can gain us an empathetic insight on the thinker's configuration of ideas. Could we have the pleasure of hearing from you snippets from the dialectical orchestration of your biography and idea, specifically on Joyce, Derrida, and Coetzee and/or South African literature?*

ATTRIDGE: I've been indulging in this orchestration in reply to some of your earlier questions, but perhaps this is an opportunity to dig deeper. But let me say first that I find philosophical biography both fascinating and troubling—fascinating because it's always interesting to know how someone who produced important abstract ideas actually lived in the material world and because, as you say, it can help in our understanding of those ideas, troubling because it can so easily be used as a way of shutting down on the ideas themselves, making them merely the outcome of a particular personality or a particular event in the individual's life or a particular historical context. One of the most interesting exemplifications of philosophical biography which is at the same time an exploration of philosophical biography is Kirby Dick and Amy Ziering Kofman's film *Derrida*. The film follows Derrida as he goes about his daily life, leaving his house, deciding what to wear for an interview, filling his pipe, teaching, and so on. There are also several sequences in which Derrida is interviewed, particularly about this very question of philosophers' lives (including his own). When the interviewer asks, "If you were to watch a documentary about a philosopher—Heidegger, Kant, or Hegel—what would you want to see in it?" Derrida answers, "Their sex lives." By way of explanation, he poses further questions: "Why do philosophers present themselves asexually in their work? Why have they erased their private lives from their work? Or never talked about anything personal?" At the same time, fully aware of the self-contradiction, Derrida himself becomes rather coy when he is asked a personal question about his first meeting with his wife. (I should add that I enjoyed the recent biography of Derrida by Benoît Peeters very much—it gave me an even stronger sense of Derrida's frailties and struggles than I had obtained from knowing him—but I don't think it advanced my understanding of his ideas, as ideas, at all.)

My secondary school was (as it had to be in South Africa at the time) an all-white school, and it prided itself on its sports rather than its academic achievements. I wasn't especially aware of my developing interest in literature and philosophy as something out of the ordinary; my ambition was directed more to the rugby and cricket fields and athletics—I excelled at sprints, long jump, and triple jump. But now I look back, I suppose I did do some unusual things, not because I was prompted but out of sheer curiosity and enjoyment; I remember reading Bertrand Russell's *History of Western Philosophy* when I must have been about fifteen and writing a review of *David Copperfield*, my first experience of Dickens (and a thrilling one), around the same time. While on a beach holiday with my parents, I came across a bargain-priced edition of Shakespeare's collected plays and spent my pocket money on it: I can still see the small and slightly fuzzy print in two columns on the cheap paper. I devoured the plays, though I can recall being very puzzled at the sexual allusions in *Measure for Measure* and *Pericles*. (This was a time of great innocence—certain pages of *The Cruel Sea* and *Moulin Rouge* were the nearest I came to an encounter with erotic literature...) The poetry of Dylan Thomas in particular fascinated me, and among the books I bought with school prizes was his *Collected Poems*. I suspect none of my peers at school shared these passions; I certainly don't remember discussing them with anyone.

I've already mentioned my enjoyment of Latin scansion at school and my pursuit of my interest in poetic form at the University of Natal and then at Cambridge. This interest went along with an interest in literary theory, though few of my teachers had similar leanings. At Natal, I was lucky enough to take philosophy classes with a lecturer, Anna Conradie (if I remember her name correctly), who had studied in Paris, and so, in the early 1960s, I was learning, in a colonial outpost, about the thought of Merleau-Ponty and phenomenology. I majored at Natal in English and Psychology, and a small part of my education in psychology was devoted to Freud, which also stood me in good stead in later years.

But academic work at Natal was overshadowed by the continuing political crisis and the struggle against apartheid. My participation took the form of demonstrations, letters to the newspaper, and similar peaceful activities; I never joined the underground movement that was pursuing a more violent policy, though I had friends who did, some of whom went to jail or permanent exile as the price of their activities. I don't remember ever making the decision to apply to universities overseas to continue my studies; it was something that seemed, as we would now say, a no-brainer. Why wouldn't you escape, the moment you could, from a society in which your relations with people of a different skin color were legally constrained, where you weren't free to read what books or newspapers you chose, where you heard every day about police violence, banning orders, and arrests for "immorality"? So my arrival in Cambridge was a moment of huge release and relief, and I eagerly bought the books I had been prevented from reading and went to lectures by exiled activists and mingled with my fellow countrymen and women of all colors. I found British politics at first very tepid—the opposing sides seemed almost indistinguishable in their policies compared to the huge disparities that characterized the South African political scene—and I found my fellow students (and later my colleagues) often strangely apolitical. Although I have always resisted the instrumentalization of literature in the name of some prior political goal, I have nevertheless always been aware that literature as a practice occurs within a context that is political as well as cultural and that a full account of literary practice needs to pay attention to this aspect.

At Cambridge, where I studied for five years, I was exposed to a much wider range of critical approaches to literature, including Leavis, Williams, Heath, Culler, Graham Hough, Muriel Bradbrook, and Jeremy Prynne. There followed two years as a research lecturer at Christ Church, Oxford, where Christopher Butler was a supportive colleague and I gave classes on stylistics, and then a lectureship at Southampton, a professorship at Strathclyde, and a move to the United States to spend ten years at Rutgers. This was an immensely stimulating decade; I had terrific colleagues (among them Michael McKeon, Michael Warner, Wai-Chee Dimock, Bruce Robbins, George Levine, and Carolyn Williams) and equally terrific graduate students and benefited enormously from the intellectual exchanges I participated in. For eight further years, I visited Rutgers twice a year to continue working with graduate students. In the meantime, thanks to a generous award from the Leverhulme Foundation, I had returned to the UK and taken up a professorship at the University of York. (I seriously considered an offer I received from Cambridge, but although as a young academic the idea of a Cambridge chair would have been beyond my wildest dreams, when it became a reality, I decided—perhaps it was a decision in Derrida's sense, a decision of the other in me, after extensive calculation left me on the horns of an undecidable dilemma—that York had a more exciting group of scholars and critics and didn't suffer from the inward-looking, self-congratulatory atmosphere that can hamper intellectual work at Oxford and Cambridge.) I've never regretted that decision; York has provided a stimulating environment for sixteen years now, and I have been able to pursue my thinking about and writing on poetry, Joyce studies, literary theory, and South African literature with constant support and encouragement. Recognition in 2008 by the government's official assessment body that York had the best English department in the country for research was only the visible registration of what I felt from my own experience to be the case.

Does any of this help to explain the attraction Derrida, or Joyce, or Coetzee exerted on me? I suppose that early fascination with the power of language, in poetry, in the theater, stayed with me, so I have always been drawn to writers, like these three, who handle language with exceptional skill. I've always valued clarity in expression, and although to many this will seem at odds with my liking for Derrida, I find his writing at its best excitingly precise even while it pushes at the boundaries of thought—much more precise than, say, the writing of Deleuze, Badiou, or Agamben, where assertion often takes the place of argument.

My interest in South African literature arises, quite obviously, from my early years there; I continued to read South African literature after leaving the country, though for decades, it never occurred to me that it could become a subject I could teach or one I would take as a subject for articles and books. In 1987—I was visiting Rutgers for the year—I was invited to join a panel at the MLA on "Canonical Reconsiderations: Class, Colonies, Gender," and having recently read and been deeply impressed by Coetzee's *Foe*, published the previous year, I decided to take its treatment of the literary canon as my topic. Then, in 1991, I was asked by the organizer of a literature series at Seton Hall—a university not far from Rutgers—to see if I could persuade Coetzee to give a reading; he agreed not to a reading but to a question-and-answer session with me, which went very well and cemented my high impression of his intelligence and integrity. A few years later, I was given the option at Rutgers of offering a course of my choosing to seniors and thought it would be fun to teach a class on South African writing. My first-hand knowledge of the context of much of what we were reading was a bonus. And not long after that, partly in order to further my own knowledge, I proposed to a younger colleague who had also grown up in South Africa but was then a professor in Canada, Rosemary Jolly, that we coedit a book on recent South African writing, which became *Writing South Africa: Literature, Apartheid and Democracy, 1970-1995*. I had, it seemed, become a South Africanist, as well as whatever else I seemed to be. That side of my career reached what I guess was its peak with the publication in 2012 of *The Cambridge History of South African Literature*, coedited with my good friend and colleague at York, David Attwell.

BAYOT: *You invoke the "question of history" a lot in your books. You, in fact, coedited* Post-Structuralism and the Question of History *(1987). Can we say that your interest in history has something to do with your program to demythologize the perception of the (a)historical connections of post-structuralism? Were you, for example, reacting to American (Yale) deconstruction, which has been depicted or stereotyped as "reading without history"?*

ATTRIDGE: This is a fair comment, though I'm glad you refer to the "stereotype" of American deconstruction, since that label covers a great deal of different kinds of work, not all of it ahistorical. But some of it did empty Derrida's work of its acute historical sense, and the perception that deconstruction was a continuation of New Criticism under another name, at least in its relation to history, was certainly around (and became stronger in the 1990s as a new wave of historicist criticism arrived on the scene and had to distinguish itself from the dominant approaches). In Britain, the historical dimension of Derrida's work—its questioning of naive uses of historical evidence as well as its interest in the history of philosophy and in the philosophy of history—was preserved to a greater extent than in the USA. And my own interest in deconstruction was refracted through the political consciousness I have described, so I always wanted to keep historical questions in mind, even while challenging appeals to history that assumed any literary work is a simple reflection of a material reality.

My sense of the importance of history is related to my sense of what constitutes the literary. I have no problem with the use of literary works as historical evidence—the fact that there are many examples of literary works being used badly as historical evidence doesn't take away from their value when used well. Nor do I have the slightest objection to the project of situating literary practices of production and reception in historical (and social, economic, and political) contexts as part of a larger project of cultural history. But these are *historical* projects, not literary ones; even if undertaken within the institutional context of a literature department, they operate on historical principles, with historical aims and outcomes. To study the production and consumption of literary works *as literature* requires an awareness of the complex relation between historical reality and art, including an awareness of the possibility that a literary work will test and perhaps undermine purely historical explanations. I've tried to describe that relation in terms of the apprehension of the otherness that a culture at a particular historical moment has to exclude in order to sustain the modes of thinking and feeling of its members.

BAYOT: *Still on history, may I know how similar or different you intend your sense of or program for history to be from that of, say, Terry Eagleton or the Essex group (represented by Francis Barker and Peter Hulme) or the Sussex cultural materialism of Jonathan Dollimore and Alan Sinfield (back in the eighties or beyond)?*

ATTRIDGE: All the people and groups you mention have done important work, to which I am greatly indebted. I've already mentioned that our "Theory and Text" conferences at Southampton were planned partly as a counterweight to the Essex conferences on the sociology of literature, which we felt were ignoring important theoretical arguments that made it impossible to carry on with purely empirical research if one wanted to do justice to the distinctiveness of literature. Our approach was a little more closely aligned with the cultural materialism of Jonathan Dollimore and Alan Sinfield, in that they were more open to the philosophical currents emanating from France and Germany, though there were still differences of emphasis: while they felt able to ground their literary studies in an unproblematic materialism, we wanted to raise questions about such a desire for grounding itself.

Terry Eagleton has been a one-man industry, going through a series of metamorphoses from radical Roman Catholic to hard-line Marxist to latter-day Leavisite, with many intermediate stages in between, so it's hard to say anything briefly about my response to his dealings with the question of history. In the earlier work that is deeply engaged with Marxist theory, such as *Criticism and Ideology*, he made a valuable contribution to literary studies, and it's been helpful to me in setting out the claims for a certain kind of materialism that I have problems with but at the same time am drawn towards. But too often, history, or History, becomes an excuse for glib put-downs of those he disagrees with. In his more recent work, like *How to Read a Poem*, Eagleton seems to have jettisoned his materialism for a revived practical criticism with overtones of the moralism of the *Scrutiny* set.

BAYOT: *Every time I (re)encounter your work and knowing how much passionate investment you have had on the peculiar language of the literary, I have always been curious to know how you position yourself intellectually vis-à-vis the Russian Formalists, specifically Roman Jakobson (whom you used as a critical point of reference for your work in "the linguistics of writing"—in that 1986 conference at Strathclyde University and as an academic field of inquiry).*

ATTRIDGE: Russian Formalism was an early interest, which I developed at the time of my PhD research when literary stylistics was a burgeoning field, and the work of Roman Jakobson in his successive incarnations as Russian Formalist, Prague Structuralist, and American linguist has been a constant source of inspiration and frustration. I say inspiration because his work on the language of literary constituted one (or rather several) of the most important breakthroughs in the formal study of literature of the twentieth century, frustration because his positivist approach prevented him from seeing the real challenge that the practices of art presented to such positivism. I included a short discussion of his work in *Peculiar Language* because he represents the most astute and thorough attempt to extirpate from literary analysis the appeal to an indefinable "something" that had constantly appeared in earlier accounts, from Aristotle on. I argued that his attempt, like all such previous attempts, failed—an argument I pursued also in the opening talk for the Strathclyde conference you mention, published in *The Linguistics of Writing*—but that its failure was highly instructive. I find I keep returning to the famous definition of the principle of poetic language as "the projection of the principle of equivalence from the axis of selection to the axis of combination," which seems to me to capture something central about our expectations and strategies when we read poetry.

BAYOT: *Now that I've invoked the Russian Formalist connection in your work, I would like to ask you about "literariness" and literary value. May I know what is your view on the category of aesthetics or literary aesthetics? How crucial is it for one's critical practice to put "aesthetics" in the picture of "literary" studies? To put the question in another way, do you think that in this age of deconstruction and difference, aesthetics could still remain a useful paradigm for literary studies? Or has aesthetic value already become too much of a bugbear that has to be discarded once and for all?*

ATTRIDGE: I must admit that I find the term *aesthetics*, bringing with it as it does an immense body of theories, analyses, debates, and prejudices, too problematic to use with ease. No matter how one qualifies one's employment of the term, it carries an indelible association with ideas of beauty, autonomy, disinterestedness, form as separate from content, and so on. Beauty, I believe, is not central to literature (though the processes whereby beauty is created, destroyed, appreciated, or ignored may play an important part in a literary work); the autonomy and disinterestedness of the artwork are concepts that need to be strongly qualified, and form is inseparable from context— and, for me, is something that *happens*. The concept of "aesthetic form" is too invested in a notion of form as spatial and static.

Nevertheless, the debates that have swirled around the term are important ones, and Kant's treatment of aesthetic judgment in the Third Critique remains an indispensable reference point for any consideration of the operation of literature or the other arts—even though Kant's focus of attention was on nature, not art. Kant, it seems to me, raised in an unignorable way one of the central problems of responses to art: the fact that they aren't determined by preexisting conceptual schemes and hence have the appearance of being purely subjective yet take the form of universal judgments. That the realm of the "aesthetic" is *not* purely subjective and yet is not amenable to our normal conceptual-rational modes of understanding is crucial to the operation of art.

BAYOT: *Your statement that "beauty, I believe, is not central to literature" is strikingly different from the common notion people have of literature as beautiful writing. If beauty is not central to literature, what is, then?*

ATTRIDGE: In three words, singularity, invention, and alterity! You must remember that my aim is to identify what is distinctive about artistic practices, both the creation of art and our responses to it. Beauty is a cultural category—one that alters across cultures and across periods, of course—that we attribute to all kinds of objects, including natural objects. Kant was concerned to explain our judgments that certain objects are "beautiful" and took as his main subject the beauty of nature. It's true that, for certain cultures in certain periods, beauty of form has been a major requirement for the work of art, although it is always a more problematic term in literature than in music and the visual arts. Is *King Lear* beautiful? Is *Moby Dick* beautiful? In the twentieth century, the requirement for beauty in any of the arts disappeared, and we now accept as genuine art creations that earlier periods would have dismissed as merely ugly.

This is not to say, however, that *form* no longer matters. My sense of the distinctiveness of literature has everything to do with form: it's through the writer's handling of form (from individual words to sentences and stanzas to narratives stretching over hundreds of pages) that inventiveness, singularity, and alterity are manifested. Our pleasure in form—which could be a rejection of traditional forms but is still an engagement with form—is central to our experience of reading, whether or not we are conscious of it. And form needs to be understood as a process, not a static property—which is how we tend to think of beauty.

BAYOT: *An interview that I personally find very interesting and insightful is the interview with Roland Barthes conducted by Jean-Jacques Brochier (first published in* Le Magazine Littéraire *in 1975). There, Barthes was engaged to discuss the key words that had been significant to him and his work. The words foregrounded for discussion in "Twenty Key Words for Roland Barthes" were pleasure, fragment, politics, Japan, and reading, among others. We're wondering if we could have the pleasure of hearing you name and talk about the key words that define and invigorate the critical universe of Derek Attridge.*

ATTRIDGE: Hmmm…Good question! Here we go:

Literature. This has to be a key word—it names what has sustained, puzzled, invigorated, exasperated me for several decades. I don't mean just the texts that we classify with this term but what the term itself means and has meant in the past, whether it names a concept that can be exhaustively defined or, instead, a place in our discourse at which conceptuality breaks down, how it operates in our culture, where its boundaries lie (if it has clear boundaries), and so on. I find I want to use it in a way that implies an evaluation: not every text that appears on the "literature" shelf deserves the title. But this is problematic, because we clearly use the word in a nonevaluative way as well, and I'm stuck with having to add an adjective or phrase—"serious literature," "literature as art," "literature worthy of the name"—none of which is satisfactory. The best I can do is accept that the broader use of the term is perfectly legitimate but make it clear that when I use the term in a theoretical discussion, I mean it in the narrower sense. (Though in another way this sense is broader, since I'm willing to accept that works classified under other headings—"history," "philosophy," "theology," "journalism," to name a few—can also be, or can contain, literature.) It's also important to register that what "literature" names is not a fixed set of texts but is historically and culturally variable, being determined by the context operative in a particular time and place.

Work. I choose this as my second word because I can think of literature only in relation to the works which manifest it. Although, for many years, I preferred the term *text* to the term *work*, following

Barthes's influential arguments, I have for some time put the emphasis on the latter term. *Work* names both the textual object and also the labor that went into its creation, and I believe that our responses to literature involve a response to that labor (not as we might discover it through historical and biographical study but as it is manifest in the text). I want to save *text*, then, for the inert symbols of a language, seen or heard, and use *work* for the literary object these symbols constitute when a reader or listener skilled in that language and in its literary conventions engages with it. The work doesn't exist, then, as an object separate from the event of reception that brings it into being—and it is therefore as much an event as an object. (Derrida uses the term *oeuvre*, which has slightly different connotations in French, for similar purposes.)

Otherness. My understanding of literature starts with an introspective examination: what happens consistently when I read a literary work—one that I am happy to call literature in the narrower sense? (I ask the same question of other forms of art; I find in my thinking I am constantly moving between literature and the visual arts and music, even though my prime concern is literature.) The answer is that whatever affect is produced in the reading process—pleasure, sorrow, excitement, amazement, dismay, horror, satisfaction, awe, sympathy, amusement, delight—in whatever combination, it is infused with an experience of newness, of being taken into a realm I was unaware of before encountering this work. This new territory may be a mental realm of ideas, images and relationships, or an emotional realm of feelings and proclivities, or, more likely, both. That's why I need a single word to name this complex newcomer into my world; *otherness* has its problems as a term, as does the alternative, *alterity*, but they are serviceable enough. I also speak of "the other," because otherness manifests itself as a singularity, rather than as a general impression. I could use *newness*, but that term would mask the fact that otherness may in fact be something old that is being revived and revisited.

From introspection, I move to an examination of what others report of their experience of reading (and writing) literature, and although most of the time words like *otherness* and *alterity* aren't employed, the descriptions very often involve something similar. To use the term *otherness* is also implicitly to bring an ethical dimension into the picture, since that which is other *to* x is that which x excludes, and such exclusion may well have ethical consequences. All over the world, injustice is being done as a result of the fear and hate of "the other," from the USA to China to France and South Africa. I write this on January 1, 2014, when EU regulations allow for the first time the unimpeded entry of Romanian and Bulgarian citizens to Britain, having had to endure months of scaremongering by politicians and journalists about this moment, in spite of massive evidence of the benefits brought to the country by immigrants from the rest of Europe. A feeling that certain groups are other feeds conflict all over the globe—at this moment, Sunni against Shia in the Middle East, Dinka against Nuer in South Sudan, Catholic against Protestant in Northern Ireland, Jew against Arab in Israel, and many others. I'm not proposing a direct link between the openness to alterity encouraged by literary works and the exercise of generosity toward other cultures and communities (for too long literary critics have made exaggerated claims about the political efficacy of their readings), but the two are not entirely unconnected.

Singularity. I like this word because it captures the uniqueness of the literary work without implying that that uniqueness arises from a fixed, absolute, and self-present identity; rather, singularity, as I use it, denotes a distinctive constellation within a cultural field. Singularity is constituted by general codes, by differences and relations (remember Saussure: in language there are no positive terms, only differences!), not by solid and unchanging entities. The singular work (or the singular output of an author, or a group, or a period—or, for that matter, the singular phrase or metaphor) is thus open to change as the cultural context out of which it is made alters through time or across cultures. What we can call the "particular," by contrast, is an entity that is opposed to the general; it is the other side of the coin of universality. I know this object on my desk is a pencil sharpener because I can immediately relate the particular before me to the general concept "pencil sharpener" (and its difference from other pencil sharpeners can also be specified in terms of particulars). Browning's "My Last Duchess," however, I know—as a work of literature—only in my experience of it as a manipulation of cultural materials (signs, concepts, feelings, perceived rhythms, and so on). There are, it is true, other uses of the term *singularity*: there is *technological* singularity, the posited moment in the future when artificial intelligence advances beyond human intelligence (though this will certainly be a singular event if it ever happens); *mathematical* singularity, a point at which a function takes an absolute value; *cosmological* singularity, which is a region in space-time at which matter is infinitely dense. Others have used the term somewhat differently, including de Man, Deleuze, Agamben, and Badiou. Peter Hallward, in *Absolutely Postcolonial*, a book which is subtitled *Writing between the Singular and the Specific*, somewhat confusingly chooses to use *singular* to refer to an entity that has no relations outside itself and *specific* to refer to an entity that is constituted by its relations—which is exactly opposite to the way I would use the terms. My allegiance among the various uses of the term is to Jean-Luc Nancy and Derrida.

Invention. This is the third of my trio of terms that I argue are necessary to account for the literary experience: the literary work introduces otherness into the field of the same through its inventiveness in relation to the culture and its singularity in relation to all other works. It is therefore an invention—a term we associate with science and engineering but also with music (Bach wrote thirty "two-part and three-part Inventions"). Derrida's essay "Psyche: Invention of the Other" helped me see the importance of invention more widely in the world of art, stressing as he did that the moment in which the new work comes into being is also the moment at which it enters the systematic relations of the culture and becomes available for use and misuse, pastiche and parody, and further inventive acts on the part of other artists. The word's earlier meaning of *finding* (from *invenio*, I find) is relevant, too: since I argue that the otherness that is apprehended through the inventive act is not simply that which hasn't been thought or felt but rather that which is excluded by the culture in order to sustain itself. There is therefore a sense in which the artist's task is to find the fractures and tensions that may be worked on to allow that other to be perceived.

Pleasure. I include this term because it signals one aspect of the experience of art that should never be forgotten—though it often is. Whatever else the literary work does, it must give pleasure (Wallace Stevens was right!). The apprehension of otherness itself is pleasurable, though it's possible that the pleasure it provides is mixed with more negative feelings. (A horror story needs to do more than just produce terror on the part of the reader; if it doesn't, no one other than a few masochists will read it.) And there are many other kinds of pleasure that the literary work can produce—the pleasure of tension and release, the pleasure of rhythm (which is a variety of tension and release), the pleasure of recognition (the introduction of otherness can feel like the appearance of something deeply familiar though never before acknowledged or articulated), and so on.

Rhythm. It will be obvious that the question of rhythm in poetry has fascinated me since I was a boy; and beyond poetry, it exerts a fascination as well. I've always been a bit skeptical about the invocation of the "rhythm of the seasons" or the "rhythm of the blood" in talking about verse, but there can be no doubt that our lives are constantly partaking of rhythms, internal and external. My interest in rhythm is related to my insistence on the temporality of the literary work, both in the sense that it can't be divorced from the passing of historical time—it remains the "same" work only because it is constantly open to change—and in the sense that it exists as an event in a reading rather than as an object to be perceived in a single atemporal instant (which is what many accounts of reading seem to imply). To emphasize the role of rhythm in the literary work is also to bring out the part played by the physical body in our responses.

Responsibility. I first began to pay serious attention to the notion of responsibility when I read an essay by Derrida entitled "Mochlos," published in a volume emanating from a 1987 conference in Tuscaloosa, Alabama, in which I participated, a conference whose aim was to explore the implications of Kant's work, *The Conflict of the Faculties.* It was clear that Derrida, in speaking of the responsibility of the university, wanted to push the term away from its more conventional meanings to a more radical understanding of it, one that does not assume a stable ego "taking responsibility" in a straightforward, conscious way. Although Derrida didn't mention Levinas in that essay, I later realized how intimately his thinking about ethics and responsibility were linked to his response to the older philosopher, about whom he wrote one of his earliest essays. He made the term his own, however, linking it to the notion of *decision*—not the conscious act of a subject but a leap taken when all rational calculation has been exhausted—and *impossibility*, understood not as a barrier to ethics but as that which enables ethics (since the realm of the possible is the realm of the calculable and computable). These themes were developed in other works, notably in *The Gift of Death*, whose third and fourth chapters made an immense impression on me. When I tried to articulate my sense of the relation of the reader to the work of art, this conception of responsibility came to me: responsibility both for the work and for the author of the work—not as a conscious, calculated act, but as an inescapable feature of an engagement with art, making it different from an engagement with other types of artifact or with natural objects. It's not that we *take* responsibility for the works we read, talk about, and write on, but rather that our relationship to those works is *constituted* by responsibility, whether we are aware of it or not.

BAYOT: *It's wonderful to hear such an intimate account of the terms that invigorate your intellectual and even spiritual heartland. But may I know what does a responsible engagement with art really mean in reading praxis? You said* responsibility *as used by Derrida is related to the notions of decision and impossibility. What does that statement mean, again to one's actual act of reading literature and art? Would you be comfortable equating or associating the term* responsibility *with* politics *or political engagement?*

ATTRIDGE: While there certainly may be a political dimension to a responsible reading of a literary work, I wouldn't equate the two. (Just as I wouldn't equate ethics with politics, though I would argue that any worthwhile politics is based on, and fosters, ethical relations.) One's responsibility to and for a literary work is a responsibility to and for the product of an individual's (or a group's) labor, mental and often physical as well, and hence a responsibility to and for another being. But there can be no recipe or handbook for responsibility, other than the basic injunction to read with care and sensitivity, since it involves a singular response to a work that is singular—and is thus related to the making of a decision (as distinct from a calculation) and to an acceptance of the impossible. The other—whether the other person or the work of literature or the foreign culture—is, as Levinas has taught us, infinite, and hence, a wholly responsible response is impossible; this would be another of those unconditional categories, like justice, forgiveness, and so on. My responsible engagement with a work is informed by that impossible demand but is always only partial. It tries to gauge what is singular about the work (which may involve some historical research) and tries to bring that singularity into the frame of the needs and hopes of the present. (This is where it might involve a political dimension.) It means approaching the work as far as possible without an agenda, without presuppositions, while acknowledging that the self that is reading is constituted by habits and preferences imbibed from the culture; it means striving hard to do justice to what is clear and logical in the work, while letting the work have an effect beyond its clarity and logic, an effect that operates not just on the rational mind but on the emotions, the body, the unconscious. It means not trying to be ingenious in multiplying interpretative subtleties but being honest about how the words strike one. It means being prepared to reread in the light of the responses of others. Responsible reading is what affirms and preserves the work, hands it on enriched to another generation.

BAYOT: *I would like to ask you a matter concerning the role of the critics in "literary" production. The matter concerns the significance of the profession or practice of criticism to literary production as well as the breeding ground of such production: the creative writing programs, classrooms, and workshops. I see a lot of discussion of this matter in David Lodge (and that's surely because he is avowedly an academic critic and a creative writer). And there were also cases where professional critics exerted enormous influence in literary production and valuation, to wit, Cleanth Brooks, who would be invited as a panelist in the poetry writing workshops at the University of Iowa during the fifties. That was a period when literary or cultural critics were still elite arbiters of taste as was the case of T. S. Eliot and Ezra Pound. In the case of Brooks and his coauthor, Robert Penn Warren, their presence as arbiter was even more foregrounded because of their set of "textbooks" on poetry, fiction, and, later on, drama. Considering* *your highly technical work on meter and rhythm, I personally think that you're one of the most qualified persons to comment on the literary and critical connections and intersections.*

ATTRIDGE: There has undoubtedly been a historical process of separation between literary critics and literary practitioners. It's hard to think of recent "creative" writers (I hesitate to use the word *creative* in this way, as I believe critics can be just as creative, but let that pass) who have had the same impact on criticism and critical theory as Matthew Arnold, Henry James, or T. S. Eliot (or, with something of a time lag, Virginia Woolf); equally, there are probably no critics or literary theorists today who have had an impact on creative writers as great as that of Arthur Symons, T. E. Hulme, or F. R. Leavis. This divide is related to the divide that has grown up between academic literary writing and more popular forms of criticism, such as newspaper and magazine reviews. In part, the growing separation of these worlds of discourse is due to the diminution in importance of *evaluation* in academic studies (a diminution associated with the rise of cultural studies), so that the task of assessing what is worth reading among the mass of works being produced every year devolves upon the more journalistic critics—who thereby have a much closer connection with the practice of writing. Some creative writers, of course, are familiar with, and influenced by, developments in literary theory—David Foster Wallace, J. M. Coetzee, and Tom McCarthy would be three examples—but many are only too ready to pour scorn on what they see as rarified, pretentious, overcomplex theorizing. Both these divisions are regrettable. I see no reason why academic criticism shouldn't be evaluative, and I don't believe that a highly technical or allusive language is necessary for many critical tasks. (This is not to say that philosophical discussions of art have to be accessible to lay readers; important advances may well need complex vocabulary and hard-to-follow argumentation. But there have always been skillful popularizers who can present at least the major consequences of philosophical argumentation.)

Having said this, I would qualify it by insisting that there remains some degree of interresponsiveness between literary writing and literary criticism and theory. The writers who achieve prominence, among the thousands whose work is published (and don't forget that much of it is highly praised by reviewers), are generally those found to be worth more considered attention in academic journals and books. This point goes back to my comments on responsibility: as readers and critics, informal and well as formal, we are responsible for the survival of literature. When I started publishing articles on J. M. Coetzee, he was a relatively little-known South African author, and though I have no evidence whatsoever that my publications had an impact on his reputation, they formed part of an increasing number of articles and later books published on his fiction, and that degree of critical attention was certainly a factor in bringing his work to the attention of the Nobel Prize Committee. The award of the prize made him one of the best-known writers in the world—so much so that now I feel it's important to divert some of the attention one might give to his work to the quality and timeliness of other writers. Coetzee may be the best novelist writing in English today—he would certainly be a candidate for that honor, though I'm not quite sure what it would mean—but not to the extent that his vastly greater exposure in both journalistic and academic media would imply.

I proposed a volume on South African literature for the Cambridge *Histories* series partly because I wanted to bring the world's attention to the many other fine writers the country has produced (and partly as a contribution to the country's reevaluation of its cultural heritage as it learns to function as a multilingual, multiracial entity based on equality rather than oppression). And this is one reason why I've been writing essays on other South African writers of whom I think highly, such as the novelist and short-story writer Zoë Wicomb; I'm involved in the editing of a collection of essays on her work, which has grown out of a series of three international conferences my colleagues and I organized. I'm currently planning to write more about Afrikaans writers and the issue of the translation of their work into English; this project is partly motivated by my sense that there are extraordinary writers who, because they choose to write in a minority language, are barely known outside South Africa.

Equally, literary writers do continue to influence literary theory, both by producing works that demand reassessment of current thinking and by their comments on literary practice. Coetzee,

McCarthy, Zadie Smith, Ngũgĩ wa Thiong'o, Julian Barnes, and Marilynne Robinson and many others have written influentially on literature in recent years. I would regard it as highly regrettable if the fact of someone's being best known as a creative writer were to preclude their recognition as a critic or theorist, though this doesn't mean the one role automatically authorizes the other one. Literary criticism, scholarship, and theory require certain areas of knowledge, familiarity with a particular type of discourse, and a specific kind of talent that aren't necessarily possessed by the creative writer, however successful.

As far as the study of meter and rhythm is concerned, one of the greatest satisfactions of my career has been to learn that poets have found my work useful. Of course, many poets find it anything but helpful to be made aware of the mechanics of what they do, preferring to work by instinct. Some, however, are very conscious of the resources the language offers them and of the possibilities of poetic form that those resources present. For instance, I have in the last couple of years had some highly fruitful conversations with Don Paterson—fruitful for me, certainly, and, if I'm to believe him, fruitful for him too. Apart from informal conversations in person and via e-mail, we have conducted a more formal interview shortly to be published in a collection in his work and have talked about a longer exchange in future that might become a book. Paterson is another example of a writer who has made an important contribution to literary theory and criticism (and, as poetry editor for Picador, plays a direct role in the promotion of particular poets at the inevitable expense of others). I'm about to write an essay on the use of rhythm in children's poetry, and I would be delighted if one or more poets writing for children in the future found my account useful.

BAYOT: *Having heard your thoughtful discussion of the material dimension of poetry (e.g., rhythm and meter) and the significance of evaluation in academic criticism to "literary" writing (e.g., poetry), I've gotten very interested in how a "technical" critic like you would put the two (materiality and evaluation of poetry) together. Would it be possible for you to demonstrate to us how such a critical approach can be enacted in a favorite poem of yours, for example?*

ATTRIDGE: Put my money where my mouth is, you mean? It's a reasonable request, given how much I've been sounding off about the right kind of criticism. But I will stress first that my argument about the value of a singular response to the singularity of the work—what Derrida calls the counter-signature to the work's signature, which both affirms it and brings it into being *as* singular—means that no critical reading on these lines is intended to be the first word or the final word; that is, it doesn't necessarily uncover hidden features that have lain undetected since the work was published, nor does it claim to have exhausted all that needs to be said. (Much criticism has one or both of these as unspoken assumptions.) I can't say that it is not exemplary, since singularity implies exemplarity: its openness to appropriation and imitation is the necessary consequence of its partaking of general norms and codes (without which it would be unreadable). But it's not offered as the only way to respond; it is one way, arising from the experience of the work in a particular place and time (though it may also incorporate memories of responses on previous occasions). And I'm going to write a little about it without carrying out any of the research into its original context that I would normally undertake before committing myself in print and without testing my response against any other critic's. I will, however, use the Oxford English Dictionary, an invaluable aid to literature of the past.

I've chosen a short poem by George Herbert, partly because it is short and partly because it is a remarkable technical achievement and you've asked me to talk about the relation between technical analysis and evaluation. It's also a religious poem, which raises interesting issues when it's being read by an atheist like myself. I've used modernized spelling and punctuation; it can be useful to read a poem like this as it originally appeared (especially if one is accustomed to the conventions of the period so the work doesn't appear quaint or unclear), but I don't think we should be fetishistic about such matters.

Virtue

Sweet day, so cool, so calm, so bright,
The bridal of the earth and sky:

The dew shall weep thy fall tonight,
      For thou must die.

Sweet rose, whose hue, angry and brave,
Bids the rash gazer wipe his eye:
Thy root is ever in its grave,
      And thou must die.

Sweet spring, full of sweet days and roses,
A box where sweets compacted lie:
My music shows ye have your closes,
      And all must die.

Only a sweet and virtuous soul,
Like seasoned timber, never gives;
But though the whole world turn to coal,
      Then chiefly lives.

When I read the title, I'm given an idea to hold onto in moving through the poem, but its relevance isn't immediate on a first reading (and every reading to some degree repeats the experience of a first reading). The poem starts with the simplest possible evocation of a perfect day, four phrases all made up of monosyllables matching the four repeated metrical units of the line, with only the foregrounded word "Sweet" diverging from the rising iambic rhythm and a simple consonantal pattern at the beginnings of words: S - d - s - c - s - c - s - b. No verbs, just a series of adjectives, the very general idea of "sweetness" immediately given some precision in relation to temperature, wind, and light. In a cold climate, one might have expected "warm" rather than "cool" as representing the perfect day (I grew up in a subtropical climate, so a cool day was often a blessing), but "cool" goes well with "calm" (not just because of the alliteration) to suggest moderation, and "bright" counters any tendency to imagine overcast weather.

    The metaphor of the second line enhances the sense of perfection, with "bridal" perhaps in the early seventeenth century retaining something of its meaning of "wedding feast" and so suggesting a celebratory event more fully than "marriage" or "wedding." This is not, in other words, one of any number of pleasant days but a unique experience of harmony. The second line also clinches the metrical pattern set up by the first: the poem is in four-beat lines, the simplest meter in English, and so far, the lines are regularly iambic (the unstressed "of" easily carrying the beat in this rhythmic context). The two lines constitute an address, the conceit of a speaker speaking to the day.

The change of mood in the third line is sudden. This line is again monosyllabic and metrically very regular, but the simplicity of the form matches a different simplicity of meaning: perfection comes to an inevitable end. The conceit of the dew mourning the disappearance of the day contributes both a clever personification—perhaps one has to be attuned to metaphysical poetry not to find it a bit *too* clever—and a new set of sensory images, damp and dark (the "fall" of "nightfall") instead of bright. There is no cleverness about the last line, which couldn't be more brutal. The four-beat line is cut down to two beats, adding to the abruptness of the statement and creating an unexpected silence as the stanza ends. Though unexpectedly short, the line rhymes with the second line (signaled by the indentation), producing a simple *abab* rhyme scheme.

There is a particular kind of pleasure in repetition-with-a-difference, and when I move on to the second stanza, I quickly realize that this is what is happening: another instance of beauty, another instance of sweetness. Now it's the traditional image of the rose—probably the red rose, though we're not told this. But there is a surprise: in contrast to the calm day, we have a color so intense that it can be called "angry" and "brave" (not "courageous" but, as the *OED* tells us, "splendid, showy, grand, fine, handsome") and so vivid that if you unwisely look at it too hard you will feel you've been hit in the face. Another conceit then, but a highly energetic one, made all the more lively by the dislocation of the rhythm, no longer smoothly unfolding as it did in the first stanza. All goes well until I reach the word "angry," which is trochaic instead of iambic and is thus given a disruptive force that underlines its meaning. It's a variation that is still within the norms of the iambic tetrameter—inversion after a syntactic break—but a jolt nevertheless. The next line is also appropriately irregular: starting with an inversion, something very common in iambic meter, it then hits us with an unexpected stressed monosyllable—"rash"—where an unstressed syllable is expected. (If we rewrite the phrase a little, the irregularity of the line becomes obvious: "Bids the observer...") We thus have a line with five strong stresses, the natural pronunciation of the words pulling against the demands of the meter. It's something of a relief to return to the iambic regularity of the next two lines, though the message is again grim: the beauty of the rose can't last, the earth that gives sustenance to the flower is also its place of death.

What now? A third example? One more of the same type would start to be boring, so Herbert, while sustaining the repetitive structure, does something different. Both days and roses are encompassed by a season: spring (now we know why the day is "cool"). Again, the rhythm is appropriate: six stressed words contribute to the fullness of the line, though there is nothing like the disruption of the previous stanza since that word "sweet"—which is beginning to cloy a little— has been repeated too often to demand a strong emphasis. The noun "sweets" in the metaphor of the second line could mean "delights" or, more concretely, sweet things to eat; the image of the box suggests the latter.

At this stage, the reader might anticipate a problem: the day ends, the flower dies, but the spring turns into summer...Herbert has a trick up his sleeve, however. All of you must die, and the evidence is in my poem: "My music shows ye have your closes." In other words, look how my stanzas end, not just with the idea of death but with the dying away of my four-beat lines into two-beat conclusions. These are the "closes" or final cadences of my stanzas, just as musical sections end with harmonic cadences. My dying falls enact those of all living beings. Poetic form has now become part of the poem's argument. For the third time, the final short line announces the inevitability of death.

After three stanzas beginning "Sweet," the opening on "Only" performs its own meaning: there is one exception to what appeared to be a universal rule. The word that was beginning to lose its force through repetition comes back once more, but this time with a complicating adjective, "virtuous," and a surprising noun, "soul." "Sweet" no longer refers to beauty apprehended by the senses (we've had visual and tactile beauty in the day and the rose, with an implication of smell in the latter, and taste and hearing in the box of sweets and in music) but to the beauty of goodness—for Herbert, Christian goodness, but the poem doesn't specify, and we needn't confine it in this way. This line returns to the regularity of the opening line of the first stanza, and the rest of the stanza follows suit. The meter may be regular, but the imagery is startling: a vision of the entire world being consumed in a conflagration (theologically, the Last Judgment, but we can read it as referring to the destructibility of all material things), which only the virtuous soul will survive.

The word "give" presents a puzzle for modern readers (we might expect seasoned timber to be precisely timber which will give and thus survive, rather than crack), and here, the *OED* is of some help. It lists forty-nine senses for the verb "to give," most with submeanings, and among these, sense 40d, "to be affected by atmospheric influences," including "of timber, to shrink from dryness"—and Herbert's lines are quoted as an example. There is a problem, however: all the nonfigurative examples given by the *OED* involve damage caused by damp, not dryness, and the only other figurative use hinges on the word "gave" in a translation by Francis Bacon published in 1658—where the 1638 edition gives, more plausibly, "gape." So, it might be better to turn to sense 40a, "to yield to pressure or strain," a sense that is still current and clearly evidenced in the one seventeenth-century citation given by the *OED*, "If that Cable had given as the other Two did, the Ship must unavoidably have been lost."

So, virtue in a soul is like seasoning in timber, preventing it from cracking or shrinking, even under the most terrible conditions. I read the lines with the same rhythm as the previous three, but they tell a very different story: the short last line, instead of a shutting up the stanza with an abrupt dead end, as it were, uses its brevity to assert a triumphant continuation. That thrice-repeated "die" is replaced with "lives." Not only will the soul survive the global conflagration: it will actually live more fully in that context. I find the stanza moves me powerfully each time I reach it in reading the poem, as the assertion of a remarkable faith in the indestructibility of immaterial values in contrast to the fragility of matter. It's not a faith I can hold onto for very long, but in experiencing the poem as it works its way from pleasant beginning to assertive end, I can share it, thanks to Herbert's remarkable handling of poetic form.

I hope this brief account has provided some sense of how I see technical matters feeding into the experience of the poem. Of course, for most readers, much of this will be unconscious, but this doesn't prevent technique from working. In fact, one might expect awareness of the technical devices to detract from the power of the poem, like seeing the machinery that allows the magician to perform her tricks, but this is not the case. The poem works its magic, and one can admire Herbert's achievement all the more.

BAYOT: *As someone who has played an important role in literary studies for decades on both sides of the Atlantic before and after Theory, what's your assessment of the current field of literary studies? Is the change towards the paradigm of cultural studies/criticism an inevitable move? Would you consider the change for the good?*

ATTRIDGE: One can see the inevitability of the rise of cultural studies, after the increased democratization of higher education after 1960 and, associated with it, the attacks on the elitism of literary studies that went along with the rise of gender and race studies, the influence of Marxist approaches, and so on. Theoretical developments, especially the work of Foucault and, a little later, Bourdieu, provided a philosophical basis for an approach to culture that refused to make evaluative judgments between "high" and "low" culture. I certainly felt, in the 1980s, that it was time to broaden the narrow canon of literature and the other arts that had reigned for so long; I felt that film and television, for instance, deserved just as much attention as the older art forms. However, I don't think I ever believed that *all* cultural productions were equally deserving of minute attention, and once cultural studies began to edge other approaches out, I found myself in what seemed like the reactionary position of wanting to value certain works of art over others. However, what I wanted to achieve was a way of thinking about literary value that took account of the critique that had been undertaken in the name of democratization, rather than a harking back to older elitist forms of criticism. This is what I attempted in *The Singularity of Literature*, and this is what I am continuing to worry away at. There are many signs that the antievaluative, all-embracing, "come on in"(to quote the late Stuart Hall) style of cultural studies has had its day and that more and more literary theorists and critics are interested in questions of value, discrimination, aesthetics, affect, and the pleasures of reading. The important question is not whether evaluation should be part of literary criticism but what form it should take and on what basis judgments should be made. (It's also important to remember that there has always been *implicit* evaluation at work, in what are chosen as suitable subjects to write about.) Fewer critics today make the claim that by uncovering the ideological biases of literary works, you can effect a change in the unfortunate conditions under which most people live.

One also hears more and more about "world literature" these days, though that label covers a variety of different approaches. To some, it is a successor to "postcolonial studies," based on the premise that postcolonial studies have too narrow and perhaps too politically oriented a focus. To others, it is a continuation of "comparative literature" in a new guise, escaping from the traditional Eurocentrism of that discipline. It can be politically committed, when, for instance, it relates literary output to uneven global development (following Immanuel Wallerstein's world systems theory), or it can have very little political content, when it becomes a license to range over different literary traditions without attention to the power relations that impact on those traditions or their historical trajectories. It has a close relationship with translation studies, which have also expanded enormously in the past ten or fifteen years, and in some varieties, it draws on the massive program of digitization that makes it possible to search across thousands of texts in an instant.

While I'm strongly in favor of extending the horizons of what is read, particularly for those of us in the English-speaking world, I have some worries about aspects of this movement or rather this array of movements. I would not like to see postcolonial studies disappear, as this is a field in which the ethical and the political role of literature is foregrounded, and we are still living in a world that bears the scars of imperialism and colonial oppression. If world literature expands the remit of postcolonialism to encompass global inequality even more fully, I think it is a valuable development; if it empties the political out of the discussion and forgets that literature arises very differently in different parts of the world as a result of inequalities, it will be a retrograde step. As for the study of literature via digitized data banks, this seems to be an interesting project, though one which belongs more to the sociology of literature than literary criticism. Like cultural studies, it sets questions of value aside, and its purely quantitative approach has nothing to say about the singularity of the individual literary work. Academic literary study and education have had a problem for several decades: students opt to study literature because of the powerful experience of engaging with specific works, and the reading public attends to reviews in daily and weekly publications because they are concerned with the same experience, but the "research" and "scholarship" we undertake often ignores this central dimension (except by implication, in choosing to write about this or that writer who in most cases, we must presume, they have enjoyed reading).

A question that often comes up in discussions of the state of literary studies today is "What happened to Theory?" During the 1980s, many literature departments were riven by fierce battles over the teaching of what everyone called Theory (the upper case signifying its difference from mere "literary theory" or "poetics," which already featured on many syllabi), and eventually no respectable English department lacked a course for undergraduates introducing a series of "approaches," feminist, deconstructive, Marxist, psychoanalytic, etc. When I started teaching, many departments, including my own, had a compulsory class on Anglo-Saxon, and this was the particular target of defiant students and faculty who objected to being forced to learn an ancient language and wanted instead to study Theory. And what has happened now? The obligatory Anglo-Saxon classes have gone, and in their place are obligatory Theory classes—and they are the classes that are now the object of the students' ire. A common complaint is "I came here to study works of literature, not abstract theories!" The successfully achieved goal of student activism in the 1980s has become the bane of many students' academic lives. And they have a point: I've always been against teaching theoretical "approaches," as if they were sitting on supermarket shelves for students to pick out what they take a liking to; I much prefer teaching theoretical issues through literary works or through the significant issues they raise.

However, this change in the pedagogic situation doesn't mean the Theory of the 1980s has gone away; rather, it has become part of the landscape–often simply a ritual obeisance to this or that famous name, but sometimes genuinely providing a more sophisticated, self-reflexive understanding of a work or a literary issue. We don't often hear any more the charge that a decade or two ago made grown men quail: "Your essay is untheorized!" But it is the case that a great deal of what gets written today—and what gets large amounts of funding—is in fact undertheorized, an accumulation of facts without a posing of hard questions about the rationale and value of what is being done. (This is one of the results of the increasing insistence in universities, in the U.K. at least, that humanities departments produce something that might be recognizable as "research" in science departments, preferably with measurable results outside the academy.) It was on account of the apparent dwindling of the legacy of Theory, and the chorus of "Theory is dead" to be heard in certain quarters (usually with a sigh of relief) that Jane Elliott and I organized a conference in 2006 with the title "Theory after 'Theory,'" and subsequently co-edited a volume of essays for Routledge with the same title. What we hoped to show was that the insights and energy that characterized the moment of "grand theory" were still very much with us, but in many new forms, often more directly involved in political action and social commitment. Our contributors to both the conference and the book ranged widely across a number of topics, including the notion of the person, the practice of war, the operation of swarms, the role of aesthetics, and the function of judgment, but in every case revealed the continuing generative power of theoretical thought descended from the innovations of the last quarter of the twentieth century.

BAYOT: *What do you think is the function of literary criticism?*

ATTRIDGE: A big question, worthy of a book (and there have been many books on it). I would rather talk in terms of functions in the plural.

I've already suggested that one function is a very traditional one that had, for a while, almost disappeared from view in the academic arena: evaluation. Criticism has the task of identifying in the extensive array of new work what is most inventive and singular, what brings into the light occluded ideas and feelings, what gives most pleasure to the reader willing to read attentively and creatively. In the case of older work, criticism may assist in the recovery of forgotten work that should not have been forgotten or expose the weaknesses of overvalued work. (Such recovery or exposure does not imply that these values are absolute or permanent; they are always in relation to the needs and values of the present, and as these change, so the valuation of works of the past change.) In doing this, criticism may open doors for writers, provide them with new models, warn them of paths not to be followed, prod them into creative emulation.

The best criticism enhances the experience of the reader, and it can do this in many different ways—illuminating the context in which the work was written, providing useful factual information, establishing a reliable text, relating the work to other works it is responding to or reacting against, inviting the reader to share the critic's experience of the work's singularity and inventiveness. The best criticism is always singular and inventive itself, springing not from a claimed universal perspective but from an acknowledged contextually situated position. As I said earlier, its fidelity to the work always involves a certain infidelity, therefore; otherwise, it would merely be repeating the work. It can also challenge the reader by pressing at the limits of acceptable interpretation, forcing him and her to justify a preferred reading.

BAYOT: *Do you foresee any change in the critical fashions—is it for better or for worse?*

ATTRIDGE: As I've suggested, I see cultural studies losing steam and many signs of a return to a sense of literature as valuable because of the demands it makes, a sense that there are—for a given time and place—better and worse works or works that criticism can reveal to be better or worse. This involves a return to careful attention to formal features and the way they operate as part of the work's meaning—or rather, part of the event of the work's meaning. I've discussed this trend in a chapter of *Moving Words* I alluded to earlier, one I titled "A Return to Form?" There is also a greater willingness to regard criticism as a report on particular experience rather than a generalizing analysis made from a height and to take seriously the importance of the pleasure afforded by literary works. I welcome all these shifts, and I see signs of these new attitudes not only in younger critics such as Ronan McDonald, Robert Eaglestone, and Krzysztof Ziarek but also in some who two or three decades ago might have been less welcoming of them, such as Isobel Armstrong, Terry Eagleton, Catherine Belsey, Kiernan Ryan, and Rita Felski.

However, these tendencies have to work against the pressure academics are currently under to shape humanistic research on the model of scientific research, so we see huge rewards given to those who assemble in teams and carry out "objective" studies of large quantities of data. The very word *research*, which has become a mantra in university circles, distorts what many of us do or want to do. This is pressure we must resist if literature and the arts more generally are to thrive; it creates an even greater divide between creative literary activity and academic studies.

BAYOT: *Do you consider your being a critic a personal decision, or a vocation, or an infliction (as Harold Bloom considers his being a critic to be)?*

ATTRIDGE: Certainly not an infliction (nor an affliction); to call it a vocation sounds rather grand, but I suppose that's what it is, since I don't recall any moment at which I made a conscious decision to pursue literary criticism. I regard it as an immense privilege to have spent a large proportion of my time over the past forty years reading literary works, thinking about them, talking about them with others equally involved, and writing about them.

When I reflect on my personal trajectory as your questions are encouraging me to do, I'm struck by the huge differences between the world of literary studies I entered in the 1960s and the world a young person bent on a similar career enters today. I hope that the choice is still, more than anything else, a vocation, a path chosen out of a sense that literary works offer unparalleled riches to those who dedicate their lives to them, and that to study and teach literature brings its own rewards. But the increasing professionalization and bureaucratization of every aspect of academic life and the diminishing availability of full-time permanent jobs teaching literature mean that the choice now has to be much more self-conscious than it was for me. When I was a graduate student at Cambridge, neither I nor any of the fellow students I was acquainted with had any idea that we might attend conferences while still working on the PhD, let alone speak at them, and publication was even further removed from our intentions. (There were, in any case, far fewer conferences and far fewer venues for publication.) I knew I wanted a post in an English department teaching literature, and once I had secured that (having rapidly made myself a specialist in Romantic literature in order to work at the same university as my then wife), I threw myself into teaching. I had no thought of publication or promotion; those seemed like things I would start considering at some distant point in the future. One of my Cambridge supervisors, W. Sidney Allen, happened to be on the editorial board of Cambridge University Press and asked if I would mind if he showed my PhD thesis to his colleagues. This took me by surprise, as I had not thought my thesis worth publication—it wasn't the study of Elizabethan love poetry I had planned—but I certainly had no objection. The result, after some revision, was my first book, published in 1974. Having published a book by accident, as it were, I gave little consideration to further publication for several years; only in 1979 did I find myself responding to a performance of Tony Harrison's *Phaedra Britannica* by writing about the couplet on the English tragic stage, which became my first article—the one I mentioned earlier that is now part of *Moving Words*. I was slowly pursuing my ideas about English prosody, and when these had reached the form of a book, I was invited to extract a section for publication as an article, which was only my second.

So, if the thirty-eight-year-old Derek Attridge had been asked to provide a CV in 1983 (one didn't keep a CV constantly up-to-date as one is advised to do now), it would show only four publications, about ten conference papers and invited lectures, and a great deal of teaching, of Romantic literature, Renaissance literature, modern literature, and stylistics. Around this time, my head of department suggested that my name might be put forward for promotion to senior lecturer, something that had not occurred to me. Then, before I knew it, I was being invited to apply for a professorship at Strathclyde University by Colin MacCabe. Looking back on these ten years now, it seems a curious start to a professional career and one that would be impossible today. I would have to have exhibited a great deal more ambition and a willingness to sing my own praises, and before I had even completed my PhD, I would have to have begun the process of presenting conference papers, publishing reviews and articles, applying for grants, and doing as much networking as I could. There's no turning back the clock, and of course, I now do all I can to assist my own students as they negotiate this rocky and tortuous path, but I regret the passing of a time when what mattered most was a dedication to literature and to sharing the pleasures and insights it offers.

BAYOT: *Do you see yourself as an heir to a particular (school of) critic, such as Roman Jakobson, for instance?*

ATTRIDGE: Well, I guess my earlier account of the influences on my work as a critic and theorist gives a picture of someone who has drawn on various schools of criticism and individual critics, so the answer must be no, I don't see myself as the heir to a single school. I don't underestimate my early exposure to the work of the New Critics (I discovered Brooks and Warren's *Understanding Poetry* in the university library when I was an undergraduate in Pietermaritzburg and devoured it: it was the first book I had come across that carried out the kind of close analysis of poems I enjoyed without the moralization of the Leavis-inspired teaching I was receiving in the English department). This influence was complicated by my growing interest in literary theory, in particular theories influenced by linguistics; Jakobson was certainly important here, as was Noam Chomsky, whose early work (*Syntactic Structures, Aspects of Syntax,* and, with Morris Halle, *The Sound Pattern of English*) made a strong impact on me. Following on from this was exposure to French post-structuralism, which made me revise my unquestioning acceptance of a scientific approach to literature. At the same time, I have continued to read analytic philosophy, and I suspect the project of thinking—and writing—as clearly and logically as possible that animates most analytic philosophers, whatever topic they are addressing, rubbed off on me. But of course, there were many other critics and theorists who I found valuable, and there were also the literary artists whose work pushed me to account for the remarkable effects they had on me.

I'm conscious of the fact that my intellectual career appears to be fractured into diverse, unconnected spheres—poetic form, literary theory, South African writing, and James Joyce. If there is something that links these, it's the interest in literary language that I've already mentioned, whether from the point of view of poets' handling of language, novelists who use language creatively, or the theoretical question of literariness. But the reason for this diversity must have something to do with the sense of excitement I feel each time a new area for study opens up—I have felt this when immersing myself in Romantic poetry in preparation for my first full teaching job, when taking on Joyce as a subject for teaching and criticism, when moving onto South African literature, when embarking on an examination of Ancient Greek and Latin poetry for my current long-term project on poetic performance, and most recently in discovering the richness of Afrikaans literature. Each time, it's like finding a new country to explore.

Perhaps I can approach the question of critical "schools" from another angle: a friend and colleague I esteem highly, Benita Parry, once said to me—we were having an extended correspondence about Coetzee's fiction, about which we had some strong but profitable disagreements—that if she were to write about my criticism, it would be under the heading, "The critic as lover of the text." In other words, she found me too much in thrall to the works I wrote about, too eager to respond to what was powerful and effective about them, whereas her criticism was dedicated to ferreting out their ideological misdemeanors. So, although there is no particular school you could say I belong to, I do align myself with a long tradition of criticism that sees its primary task as investigating and championing literary works it believes are worth such attention, rather than inspecting works in order to expose their complicity with capitalism, sexism, homophobia, or racism. Of course, concentrating on the best means ignoring the worse (or, sometimes, showing in what ways the worse are worse), so there is a negative as well as a positive element in this approach, but it remains very different from what became known as the "hermeneutics of suspicion," which treats works of art as effects of ideology. (There's a somewhat different appeal to ideology in the approach associated with the name of Pierre Macherey, in which the great works of literature are shown to have escaped the determinations of the ideological structures of their time; I'm more sympathetic to this methodology, though it seems to me there are many other reasons to value literary achievements.) This doesn't have to result in a narrow canon-focused approach; it is motivated not by a desire to keep the unworthy out of the privileged realm of the elect but by its opposite—a desire to expand the territory of worthwhile literature by creatively responding to the new, the experimental, the inventive, wherever it might appear.

BAYOT: *Who, in particular, was/is the audience you have in mind?*

ATTRIDGE: I don't think consciously about the audience for my writing most of the time; it's more a question of continually revising what I write to make it as clear as possible to myself as reader. Occasionally, I'm aware of writing for a particular audience, either a specialized one (when, for instance, contributing to a collection of essays on Derrida's work that I know will be read only by those already familiar with his work) or a general one, as in my collaboration with Tom Carper on *Meter and Meaning*, which we planned as a useful book for high school students, undergraduates, and general readers.

BAYOT: *I'm sure your readers are all grateful for the lucidity of your critical prose and that is considering that you're writing on Derrida and deconstruction. Is the writing of that kind of prose a natural thing for you or has it been a deliberate act?*

ATTRIDGE: If by "deliberate," you imagine a writer who has to tell himself to be more lucid in order to forestall, or correct, a tendency to be opaque, then I don't think it can be said to be a deliberate act. My desire to write clearly and to keep revising until the words say what I want them to say as lucidly as possible (which isn't always what I set out to say when I started) does come naturally. Earlier in my writing career, I was always surprised when readers and reviewers singled out the lucidity of my style; I wasn't aware that I was writing in a particularly clear way, and I always felt—and continue to feel—that what I produce could be more precise.

BAYOT: *Now that we're on the topic of style, I'm wondering (most likely on behalf of many readers) about, if Derrida and deconstruction can be presented in such a lucid style that you exemplify, what you think is the reason for the difficulty of Derrida's prose. Should we just accept it as a matter of his personal style? Or should we rather know that there's a discursive point for such difficulty (as against the option of lucidity)? I'm sure that as a scholar and personal friend of Derrida, you are one of the best persons to enlighten us on this point.*

ATTRIDGE: One can come at this question from a number of angles. As I've said, the quality of the English translations of Derrida's work is variable, and often, the original is easier to follow—for those who know French—than the translation. (I've already commented on my discovery, in editing *Act of Literature*, that puzzles in the English text were frequently solved by referring to the French.) But there's no doubt that even in French, much of his work makes considerable demands on the reader. One factor is the intellectual context in which Derrida wrote (and gave seminars): making everything as clear as possible for a lay audience was not a priority for Derrida's teachers, friends, and colleagues. I'm thinking of associates and contemporaries like Blanchot, Levinas, Althusser, Lyotard, Foucault, Deleuze, Sollers, Lacan, Kristeva, Nancy, Laplanche, and Lacoue-Labarthe. (Barthes was something of an exception, though not all his writing was transparent, by any means.) There was a shared background that could be assumed, a background that included familiarity with a particular group of philosophers: the German tradition of Kant, Hegel, Nietzsche, Marx, Heidegger, and Husserl and French interpreters of this tradition such as Levinas (in his early work) and Alexandre Kojève, as well as other French philosophers such as Bergson, Merleau-Ponty, and Canguilhem. (One could add Sartre, though Sartre's influence was largely subterranean.) For the literary scholar or philosopher brought up in the Anglo-American tradition, writing that assumes this background is always going to be difficult. When I embarked on a project of getting to know the work of Derrida, Kristeva, Lacan,

Barthes, and Foucault, I quickly realized that this also meant getting to know these German and French philosophers.

But another factor, perhaps the most important one, is that Derrida's writing is always pushing at the limits of the thinkable, and this is bound to produce challenges for the reader. Since part of what he wants to demonstrate is that our habitual uses of words and the assumptions crystallized in "common sense" give a false picture of reality, he has to write in such a way as to dislocate linguistic habits and thus habits of thought. To take one well-known example (one I've already touched on in referring to Martin Hägglund's *Radical Atheism*), at the heart of Derrida's philosophy is the claim that time and space are inseparable—a questioning of our assumption (which is also an assumption that undergirds virtually the whole of Western philosophy) that an entity can be wholly present to itself and that this self-presence constitutes a solid basis for thought. For Derrida, space is always becoming time; time is always becoming space. An entity is not just what it is, but the outcome of what it has ceased to be and the preparation for what it is about to become; its spatial existence is thus inescapably temporal, while its temporality is bound up with its possession of spatial properties that enable it to exist at all from one moment to another. But saying it like this is still inadequate, as it continues to imply that space and time are separate; Derrida wanted a way to convey, against the normal tendencies of language, their inseparability. One of his answers was the made-up word *différance*: a word that looks like a noun derived from the word *différer*, which means either to defer or to differ, but sounds like the word *différence*, which means only difference. A temporal property—deferring—is combined with a spatial property—differing. (The term is sometimes represented in English as "differance," but this loses the important double meaning present in the French.) The fact that the difference between *différence* and *différance* can only be registered in writing is a further part of the argument, since Derrida wants to challenge the traditional privileging of the apparent self-presence of—temporal—speech over the apparent secondariness of—spatial—writing.

Now, I wouldn't claim that the difficulty of Derrida's writing was always due to these factors; especially in his later work, he developed a style of allusive, apparently meandering, and rather wordy writing. The sense remains, however, of someone pushing at the limits of what language will allow him to say.

I often turn to Derrida's interviews for the clearest exposition of his thinking, such as the interviews with Elisabeth Roudinesco in *For What Tomorrow…*, with Maurizio Ferraris in *A Taste for the Secret*, with Giovanna Borradori in *Philosophy in a Time of Terror*, and, of course, with me in *Acts of Literature*.

BAYOT: *Having had the privilege of moving and being guided around your critical landscape, I would like to shift gears and drive to a more personal terrain of yours: your family. What were your parents like? Are/Were they readers of literature? Are/Were they supportive of your pursuit of English or literature or criticism? How about your family now—people who read your drafts and ask the hard questions (only if I may ask)?*

ATTRIDGE: My parents were fairly typical white middle-class South Africans; the books on our shelves were popular fictions (Nevil Shute, Nicholas Monsarrat), South African classics (*Jock of the Bushveld*, *Cry the Beloved Country*), middlebrow poetry (Robert Service, Rupert Brooke); the music we listened to came from Broadway or Tin Pan Alley. My father was a schoolteacher specializing in geography, later a headmaster; my mother, a housewife; I grew up in a peaceful suburb of Pietermaritzburg, a town affectionately known as "Sleepy Hollow," the third of three children. As a boy, I was more interested in sport and outdoor pursuits than intellectual pursuits—I enjoyed camping and hiking, especially in the sublime Drakensberg mountain range— but without consciously trying to "improve" myself, I did respond to the efforts of my English teachers to expand my reading. I've already mentioned my early enjoyment of modern poetry, and I did well in English essays and exams without really trying terribly hard. My parents supported and encouraged me, though they didn't have the background necessary to push me; my brother and sister (considerably older than me) were headed for careers in banking and librarianship. Pietermaritzburg in apartheid South Africa was not a cultural center, and what culture there was—the occasional concert, some interesting paintings in the art gallery—I was not capable of appreciating as a teenager. I used to go with my parents to the annual Philharmonic Society musical—*Desert Song, Brigadoon,* once or twice a Gilbert and Sullivan operetta—and I remember a performance of Handel's *Messiah* that I found impressively unlike anything I had heard before. Like the young John Coetzee, as related in his memoir *Boyhood,* a great deal of my cultural education came from perusing the several volumes of Arthur Mee's *Children's Encyclopedia.*

An event that had a powerful impact on me—it was in 1962, during my last year in high school—was my attendance at a visiting production in the university's main hall. The play was a two-hander, and one of the actors was also the author of the piece, a little-known young dramatist named Athol Fugard. Entitled *The Blood Knot,* the work examined the problems of racial classification under apartheid laws, and I found it both dramatically and politically riveting. I hadn't realized how relevant contemporary literature could be to the crucial events of my own world, since virtually everything I had read came from far away and long ago.

It wasn't until university that my eyes were opened to the wider cultural world. There were works I studied in class, of course, including new realms of English literature (largely the works endorsed by F. R. Leavis, including heavy doses of D. H. Lawrence, but I will always be grateful at having been made to read Samuel Richardson's *Clarissa* by one faculty member who had written a book on it). But more exciting was what I was discovering outside the classroom. There were conversations, for instance, with a young lecturer named Jacques Berthoud who, although he had grown up in South Africa, was from a French-Swiss family and had completed part of his schooling in Geneva; he seemed to breathe a different atmosphere from the rest of the teaching staff (he had a pronounced French accent) and could talk animatedly about classical music and European art and literature in several languages. There was a young classics lecturer, Saul Bastomsky, whom I got to know over meals in the student union; Saul was a committed Marxist who undermined many of my cherished, and somewhat naïve, political principles.

And I learned from my fellow students. Jeff Guy, for instance, who was a few years older, seemed very much a man of the world and introduced me to classical music. Another was Colin Bundy, who was more intellectually ambitious than me and prodded me into new discoveries. And Patricia Dodds, with whom I fell in love and who lent me several books that opened my eyes to European literature (I remember in particular Molière's *Don Juan*, Tolstoy's short stories, and Kafka's *The Trial*). Only later did it occur to me what a strange distortion it was that I was not encouraged by anyone in or outside the classroom to pay attention to South African writing (other than the plays of a faculty member in the English Department, which used Shakespearean language to engage with "universal" themes). In this respect, my cultural education—Fugard's *The Blood Knot* notwithstanding—was typically colonialist.

(The further careers of those who influenced me are revealing. Jacques Berthoud left South Africa shortly after I did, and we became colleagues at the University of Southampton a few years later; he then left to become head of the English department at York University, where I joined him again in 1998, to become head of department in turn, sometime after his retirement. Saul Bastomsky I last heard of as a lecturer at Monash University, Melbourne. Jeff Guy became a leading South African historian, teaching in England, Norway, and, finally, back in South Africa. Colin Bundy was awarded a Rhodes scholarship, taught history at various universities, and eventually became director of the School of Oriental and African Studies in London and then master of an Oxford college. Pat Dodds died tragically young. What if we could have been granted a glimpse of our futures when we were together in the early 1960s!)

For my first 21 years I traveled very little (a South African passport wasn't valid for most of Africa, and I didn't have the resources to go further afield), but once I had made the big move to Britain I embarked on what turned out to be a lifetime of traveling. It began in 1967, in my first summer in the northern hemisphere, with an epic journey in a tiny car (some will remember the original Mini) with three friends across Europe to Istanbul and back, including a few days in a remote Romanian village to stay with the family of a fellow member of my Cambridge college. I suspect that my frequent changes of environment since then have been intellectually fruitful, and they have certainly allowed me to encounter, and often to get to know, a number of remarkable individuals in different corners of the globe. My major relocations, after the initial departure from South Africa, were from the UK to the USA in 1988 and back to the UK in 1998; the transition from England to Scotland in 1984 was also culturally highly rewarding. I've been lucky enough to benefit from some wonderful residencies, at the Camargo Foundation in Cassis (in the south of France), at the Stellenbosch Institute for Advanced Study in South Africa (where my conversations with some brilliant writers in, and translators of, Afrikaans initiated a new direction in my intellectual trajectory), and at the Bogliasco Foundation in Italy; a Visiting Fellowship at All Souls, Oxford, was equally productive, and I'm looking forward to a similar Fellowship at St. Catherine's College and to a semester at the National Humanities Center in North Carolina. There have also been numerous shorter visits—to give talks, meet students, or participate in conferences—that have invariably been rewarding as stimulants to my thinking.

And when I reflect on the value of meeting interesting, generous individuals around the world, I realize too how important joint editorial projects have been to me, from my early collaboration with Daniel Ferrer in editing *Post-Structuralist Joyce* and with Geoff Bennington and Robert Young in producing *Post-Structuralism and the Question of History* to more recent joint efforts with Marjorie Howes on *Semicolonial Joyce,* Rosemary Jolly on *Writing South Africa,* Tom Carper on *Meter and Meaning,* Jane Elliott on *Theory after "Theory,"* and David Attwell on *The Cambridge History of South African Literature.* In every case, I have learned enormously from my fellow editor (and from our contributors). I'm currently co-editing a volume of essays on Zoë Wicomb with Kai Easton—the final stage of a project that we conceived together some five or six years ago, and one that included three conferences—and I know I will once more be stimulated and enriched by our conversations.

I haven't said much about the importance of teaching in my intellectual life, an activity whose role in my intellectual life can't be overstated. From the first classes I taught as an Honours student in psychology at the University of Natal nearly fifty years ago to my current supervising of PhD students and occasional teaching of MA classes at the University of York, teaching has been a constant source of inspiration, information and pleasure. I'll go on doing it as long as my university will allow me.

My family now for the most part lets me get on with my work, as they all live very busy lives. My wife is the deputy head of a local Quaker school, which means long hours during the school term and catching up and preparation during the vacations; my younger daughter is finishing an English degree and preparing for a graduate teacher training degree so she can become a primary school teacher; and my older daughter is a singer, undertaking postgraduate vocal studies at the Royal College of Music. I send copies of my books to my brother and sister in South Africa, with the firm message that I don't expect them to read them! The reading of drafts and the asking of hard questions comes from colleagues, though sometimes I wish their questions were tougher. (I'm currently writing a long piece in which I pose to myself the hard questions that I think should have been asked about *The Singularity of Literature*.)

BAYOT: *Whither Derek Attridge and his critical pursuit of the peculiar language of literature, if we may ask?*

ATTRIDGE: I am enjoying being semi-retired—three years ago I retired from full-time teaching and the university reemployed me on a part-time contract. My main duties are supervising PhD students and mentoring younger colleagues, which I enjoy enormously. So, I have more time to write, and I'm more able to accept invitations to speak (in the coming couple of years I'm looking forward to visits to India, Australia, China, Cyprus, South Africa, the USA, France, Italy, and possibly South Korea). I have several book projects I'm hoping to complete before too long—a follow-up to *The Singularity of Literature*, which will explore more fully some of the issues I treated rather quickly in that book and engage in more detail with other critics and philosophers; a "conversation" with Henry Staten on the reading of poetry (we're attempting to counter what we both feel is a regrettable tendency in recent literary criticism to overlook the fundamentals of careful reading in order to pursue overingenious interpretations); a collection of essays on fiction; and my long-term study of poetry as a performance art from Ancient Greece to the Renaissance (and perhaps beyond). And of course, this book. I'm on seventeen journal editorial boards, and so, I receive a stream of submitted essays to read, and publishers frequently request reports on submitted book manuscripts. With numerous former PhD students embarked on academic careers, there are always references to write, requests for reports on faculty members up for promotion in American universities keep coming in, and colleagues in my department and at other universities often ask for my support in grant applications. I'm often involved in external examining of PhD theses at other universities in Britain and similar tasks for overseas universities. As a fellow of the British Academy, I'm involved in assessing submissions for financial support, as well as considering the work of potential fellows as part of the process of election. A great proportion of what I read is in connection with these activities.

Though I find it hard to believe, I will turn seventy in 2015— my colleagues are organizing a conference to celebrate the event, bless them—and it would be agreeable if one or two of these books were out by then. When my wife retires, perhaps I will feel retired too and spend more time reading and rereading (my bookshelves have long since given up trying to cope with my purchases, but my Kindle is now filling with books I am eager to get to), enjoying music, photography, architecture, and even more travel. On the other hand, I may not be able to stop writing...

Derek Attridge
Chronological List of Publications

I. AS AUTHOR

A. Books

The Work of Literature. Oxford: Oxford University Press, 2015.

The Craft of Poetry: Dialogues on Minimal Interpretation (with Henry Staten). London: Routledge, 2015.

Moving Words: Forms of English Poetry. Oxford: Oxford University Press, 2013. Chapter 4 reprinted in *Nordisk Samtidspoesi, Særlig Øyvind Rimbereids forfatterskap*. Ed. Ole Karlsen. Vallset: Oplandske bokforlag, forthcoming.

Reading and Responsibility: Deconstruction's Traces. Edinburgh: Edinburgh University Press, 2010. The Frontiers of Theory. Paperback edition, 2011.

How to Read Joyce. London: Granta Books, 2007 (paperback). Chinese translation in preparation.

J. M. Coetzee and the Ethics of Reading: Literature in the Event. Chicago: University of Chicago Press, 2004. Scottsville, South Africa: University of KwaZulu-Natal Press, 2005 (cloth and paperback). Chapter 8 reprinted in the *Virginia Quarterly Review* 80.4 (Autumn 2004). Extract from Chapter 1 reprinted in *A Companion to the Works of J. M. Coetzee*. Ed. Tim Mehigan. Rochester: Camden House, 2011. Polish translation of Chapter 2 published in *Wielcy Artyści Ucieczek*. Ed. Piotr Jakubowski and Małgorzata Jankowska. Kraków: Korporacja Halart, 2014.

The Singularity of Literature. London: Routledge, 2004 (cloth and paperback). Winner of the 2006 European Society for the Study of English Prize for literary studies. Translated into Polish as *Jednostkowość literatury*. Krakow: Universitas, 2007. Translated into Spanish as *La singularidad de la literatura*. Madrid: Abada Editores, 2011.

Meter and Meaning: An Introduction to Rhythm in Poetry (with Thomas Carper). London: Routledge, 2003 (cloth and paperback).

Joyce Effects: On Language, Theory, and History. Cambridge: Cambridge University Press, 2000 (cloth and paperback). Electronic edition, 2003 (Netlibrary and eBooks). Extracts reprinted in *James Joyce*. Ed. Harold Bloom. Bloom's Major Novelists. Broomall: Chelsea House, 2002. And *James Joyce*. Ed. Colin Milton. Critical Assessments of Major Writers. London: Routledge, 2012.

Poetic Rhythm: An Introduction. Cambridge: Cambridge University Press, 1995 (cloth and paperback).

Peculiar Language: Literature as Difference from the Renaissance to James Joyce. Ithaca: Cornell University Press; London: Methuen, 1988 (cloth and paperback). Reissued with new foreword, London: Routledge, 2004. Chapter 7 reprinted in Portuguese translation in *riverrun: Ensaios sobre James Joyce*. Ed. Arthur Nestrovski. Rio de Janeiro: Imago, 1992. Extract from Chapter 7 reprinted in *Critical Essays on James Joyce's* Finnegans Wake. Ed. Patrick A. McCarthy. New York: G. K. Hall, 1992. Extract from Chapter 5 reprinted in *Stylistics: A Resource Book for Students*. Ed. Paul Simpson. London: Routledge, 2004. Extract from Chapter 2 reprinted in *Reconceiving the Renaissance: A Critical Reader*. Ed. Ewan Fernie, Ramona Wray, Mark Thornton Burnett, and Clare McManus. Oxford: Oxford University Press, 2005. Chapter 7 reprinted in *James Joyce*. Ed. Harold Bloom. Bloom's Modern Critical Views. Broomall: Chelsea House, 2009.

The Rhythms of English Poetry. English Language Series 14. London: Longman, 1982 (cloth and paperback). Reissued, 1988.

Well-Weighed Syllables: Elizabethan Verse in Classical Metres. Cambridge: Cambridge University Press, 1974. Paperback edition, 1979. Reissued, 2008.

B. Book Chapters

"The Department of English and Experience of Literature—Present." *English Studies: The State of the Discipline, Past, Present, and Future*. Ed. Niall Gildea et al. Hampshire: Palgrave, 2015.

"Contemporary Afrikaans Fiction and English Translation: Singularity and the Question of Minor Languages." *Singularity and Transnational Poetics*. Ed. Birgit M. Kaiser. London: Routledge, forthcoming.

"Form in Poetry: An Interview between Don Paterson and Derek Attridge." *Don Paterson: Contemporary Critical Essays*. Ed. Natalie Pollard. Edinburgh: Edinburgh University Press, 2014. 75–82.

"Don Paterson's *Ars Poetica*." *Don Paterson: Contemporary Critical Essays*. Ed. Natalie Pollard. Edinburgh: Edinburgh University Press, 2014. 21–33.

"Response to Scarry and Larmore." *The Humanities in the Public Sphere*. Ed. Peter Brooks. Bronx: Fordham University Press, 2014. 62–66.

"Beat." *The Oxford Handbook of Nineteenth-Century Literature*. Ed. Matthew Bevis. Oxford: Oxford University Press, 2013. 36–55.

"Signature/Countersignature: Derrida's Response to *Ulysses*." *Derrida and Joyce: Texts and Contexts*. Ed. Andrew J. Mitchell and Sam Slote. New York: SUNY Press, 2013. 265–80.

"Posthumous Infidelity: Derrida, Levinas, and the Third." *Re-Reading Derrida: Perspectives on Mourning and Its Hospitality*. Ed. Tony Thwaites and Jude Seaboyer. Plymouth: Lexington Books, 2013. 23–39.

"Pararealism in 'Circe.'" *Joycean Unions: Post-Millennial Essays from East to West*. Ed. R. Brandon Kershner and Tekla Mecsnóber. European Joyce Studies 22. Amsterdam: Rodopi, 2013. 119–26.

"'To Speak of This You Would Need the Tongue of a God': Representing the Trauma of Township Violence." *Trauma, Memory and Narrative in the Contemporary South African Novel*. Ed. Ewald Mengel and Michela Borzaga. Amsterdam: Rodopi, 2012. 177–94.

"'Eveline' at Home: Reflections on Language and Context" (with Anne Fogarty). *Collaborative Dubliners: Joyce in Dialogue*. Ed. Vicki Mahaffey. Sycaruse: Syracuse University Press, 2012. 89–107.

"Joyce: The Modernist Novel's Revolution in Matter and Manner." *The Cambridge History of the English Novel*. Ed. Robert Caserio and Clement Hawes. Cambridge: Cambridge University Press, 2012. 581–95.

Epilogue. *Tradition, Trauma, Translation: The Classic and the Modern*. Ed. Jan Parker and Timothy Mathews. Oxford: Oxford University Press, 2011. 347–51.

"The Arbitrary." *Reading Derrida's* Of Grammatology. Ed. Sean Gaston and Ian Mclachlan. London: Continuum, 2011. 58–68.

"Coetzee's Artists, Coetzee's Art." *J. M. Coetzee's Austerities*. Ed. Graham Bradshaw and Michael Neill. Surrey: Ashgate, 2010. 25–42.

"On Knowing Works of Art." *Inside Knowledge: (Un)doing Ways of Knowing in the Humanities*. Ed. Carolyn Birdsall et al. Newcastle upon Tyne: Cambridge Scholars Press, 2009. 17–34. First printed in *Anglo-Saxonica* 26 (2008): 15–34.

"Le lieu de la déconstruction" (with J. M. Rabaté). *Derrida d'ici, Derrida de là*. Ed. Thomas Dutoit. Paris: Galilée, 2009. 159–76.

"Sex, Comedy and Influence: Coetzee's Beckett." *J. M. Coetzee in Context and Theory*. Ed. Elleke Boehmer, Katy Iddiols, and Robert Eaglestone. London: Continuum, 2009. 71–90.

"Derrida's Singularity: Literature and Ethics." *Derrida's Legacies: Literature and Philosophy*. Ed. Simon Glendinning and Robert Eaglestone. London: Routledge, 2008. 12–25.

"'C'est donc ça l'art': La figure de l'artiste dans les écrits post-apartheid de J. M. Coetzee." *J. M. Coetzee et la littérature Européenne: Écrire contre la barbarie*. Ed. Jean-Paul Engélibert. Rennes: Presses Universitaires de Rennes, 2007. 181–91.

"The Art of the Impossible?" *The Politics of Deconstruction: Jacques Derrida and the Other of Philosophy*. Ed. Martin McQuillan. Ann Arbor: Pluto Press, 2007. 54–65.

"Beckett en el Hemisferio Sur: comedia beckettiana de J. M. Coetzee." *Tentativas sobre Samuel Beckett*. Ed. Julián Jiménez Heffernan. Madrid: Circulo de Bellas Artes, 2007. 57–91.

"The Body Writing: Joyce's Pen." *Joyce, "Penelope" and the Body*. Ed. Richard Brown. European Joyce Studies 17. Amsterdam: Rodopi, 2006. 47–62.

"Against Allegory: *Waiting for the Barbarians, Life & Times of Michael K*, and the Question of Literary Reading." *J. M. Coetzee and the Idea of the Public Intellectual*. Ed. Jane Poyner. Athens, OH: University of Ohio Press, 2006. 63–82.

"Keats and Beats, or What Can We Say about Rhythm?" *Le rythme dans les littératures de langue anglaise*. Ed. Daniel Thomières. Reims: Presses Universitaires de Reims, 2005. 99–116.

"Miller's Tale." *The J. Hillis Miller Reader*. Ed. Julian Wolfreys. Edinburgh: Edinburgh University Press, 2005. 78–82.

"Encountering the Other in the Classroom: An Interview." *Thinking Difference: Critics in Conversation*. Ed. Julian Wolfreys. Bronx: Fordham University Press, 2004. 11–19.

"Suivre Derrida." *Cahiers de l'Herne: Jacques Derrida*. Ed. Marie-Louise Mallet and Ginette Michaud. Paris: L'Herne, 2004. 89–91.

"Language, Sexuality, and the Remainder in *A Portrait of the Artist as a Young Man*." *Joyce and the Difference of Language*. Ed. Laurent Milesi. Cambridge: Cambridge University Press, 2003. 128–41.

"Joyce and the Making of Modernism: The Question of Technique." *Rethinking Modernism*. Ed. Marianne Thormählen. Hampshire: Palgrave, 2003. 149–59.

"Singular Events: Literature, Invention, and Performance." *The Question of Literature: The Place of the Literary in Contemporary Theory*. Ed. Elizabeth Beaumont-Bissell. Manchester: Manchester University Press, 2002. 48–65.

"Deconstruction and Fiction." *Deconstructions: A User's Guide*. Ed. Nicholas Royle. Hampshire: Palgrave, 2000. 105–18.

"On Being a Joycean." *A Collideorscape of Joyce: Festschrift for Fritz Senn*. Ed. Ruth Frehner and Ursula Zeller. Dublin: Lilliput Press, 1998. 18–30.

"Roland Barthes's Obtuse, Sharp Meaning and the Responsibilities of Commentary." *Writing the Image after Roland Barthes.* Ed. Jean-Michel Rabaté. Philadelphia: University of Pennsylvania Press, 1997. 77–89.

"Expecting the Unexpected in Coetzee's *Master of Petersburg* and Derrida's Recent Writings." *Applying: to Derrida.* Ed. John Brannigan, Ruth Robbins, and Julian Wolfreys. London: Macmillan, 1996. 21–40.

"Avant l'arrivant: *Le Maître de Pétersbourg* de J. M. Coetzee et quelques ouvrages récents de Jacques Derrida." *Passions de la littérature.* Ed. Michel Lisse. Paris: Galilée, 1996. 323–47.

"Countlessness of Livestories: Narrativity in *Finnegans Wake.*" *Joyce in the Hibernian Metropolis: Essays.* Ed. Morris Beja and David Norris. Columbus: Ohio State University Press, 1996. 290–96.

"'Aeolus' without Wind: Introduction." *Joyce in the Hibernian Metropolis: Essays.* Ed. Morris Beja and David Norris. Columbus: Ohio State University Press, 1996. 179–80.

"Theories of Popular Culture." *Joyce and Popular Culture.* Ed. R. B. Kershner. Gainesville: University Press of Florida, 1996. 23–26.

"The Linguistic Model and Its Applications." *The Cambridge History of Literary Criticism.* Ed. Raman Selden. Vol. 8. Cambridge: Cambridge University Press, 1995. 58–84. Paperback edition, 2005.

"Singularities, Responsibilities: Derrida, Deconstruction, and Literary Criticism." *Critical Encounters: Reference and Responsibility in Deconstructive Writing.* Ed. Cathy Caruth and Deborah Esch. New Brunswick: Rutgers University Press, 1994. 106–26. Reprinted in Italian translation in *Decostruzione e/è America: Un reader critico.* Ed. Andrea Carosso. Turin: Tirrenia Stampatori, 1994. 269–86.

"Ghost Writing." *Deconstruction Is/in America: A New Sense of the Political.* Ed. Anselm Haverkamp. New York: New York University Press, 1994. 223–27. Reprinted in *Deconstruction: A Reader.* Ed. Martin McQuillan. Edinburgh: Edinburgh University Press, 2000. 175–77.

"Literary Form and the Demands of Politics: Otherness in J. M. Coetzee's *Age of Iron.*" *Aesthetics and Ideology.* Ed. George Levine. New Brunswick: Rutgers University Press, 1994. 243–63. Reprinted in *Critical Essays on J. M. Coetzee.* Ed. Sue Kossew. New York: G. K. Hall, 1998. 198–213.

"Le texte comme autre: La forme sans formalisme." *Le Passage des frontières: Autour du travail de Jacques Derrida.* Ed. Marie-Louise Mallet. Paris: Galilée, 1994. 53–55.

"Oppressive Silence: J. M. Coetzee's *Foe* and the Politics of the Canon." *Decolonizing Tradition: New Views of Twentieth-Century "British"*

Literature. Ed. Karen Lawrence. Champaign: University of Illinois Press, 1992. 212–38. Revised version printed in *Critical Perspectives on J. M. Coetzee*. Ed. Graham Huggan and Stephen Watson. London: Macmillan, 1996. 168–90.

"Reading Joyce." *The Cambridge Companion to James Joyce*. Ed. Derek Attridge. Cambridge: Cambridge University Press, 1990. 1–30. Reprinted in *Modern British Literature*. Ed. Laurie Di Mauro. Farmington Hills: St. James Press, 1999. Reprinted in Polish translation in *Literatura na świeci* 7–8 (2004): 32–67. Extract reprinted on *Fathom*. Columbia University, n.d. <fathom.com>.

"Linguistic Theory and Literary Criticism: *The Rhythms of English Poetry Revisited*." *Phonetics and Phonology: Rhythm and Meter*. Ed. Paul Kiparsky and Gilbert Youmans. San Diego: Academic Press, 1989. 183–99.

"The *Wake*'s Confounded Language." *Coping with Joyce: Essays from the Copenhagen Symposium*. Ed. Morris Beja and Shari Benstock. Columbus: Ohio State University Press, 1989. 262–68.

"Criticism's Wake." *James Joyce: The Augmented Ninth: Papers from the Ninth International James Joyce Symposium*. Ed. Bernard Benstock. Syracuse University Press, 1988. 80–87.

"Joyce and the Ideology of Character." *James Joyce: The Augmented Ninth: Papers from the Ninth International James Joyce Symposium*. Ed. Bernard Benstock. Sycaruse: Syracuse University Press, 1988. 152–57.

"Unpacking the Portmanteau, or Who's Afraid of *Finnegans Wake*?" *On Puns: The Foundation of Letters*. Ed. Jonathan Culler. Oxford: Blackwell, 1988. 140–55.

"Closing Statement: Linguistic and Poetics in Retrospect." *The Linguistics of Writing: Arguments between Language and Literature*. Ed. Nigel Fabb et al. Manchester: Manchester University Press, 1987. New York: Routledge, 1988. 15–32. Reprinted in *The Stylistics Reader: From Roman Jakobson to the Present*. Ed. Jean Jacques Weber. London: Edward Arnold, 1996. 36–53.

"Language as History/History as Language: Saussure and the Romance of Etymology." *Post-Structuralism and the Question of History*. Ed. Derek Attridge, Geoff Bennington, and Robert Young. Cambridge: Cambridge University Press, 1987. 183–211.

"Joyce's Lipspeech: Syntax and the Subject in 'Sirens.'" *James Joyce: The Centennial Symposium*. Ed. Morris Beja et al. Urbana: University of Illinois Press, 1986. 59–66.

"Puttenham's Perplexity: Nature, Art, and the Supplement in Renaissance Literary Theory." *Literary Theory/Renaissance Texts*. Ed. Patricia Parker and David Quint. Baltimore: Johns Hopkins University Press, 1986. 257–79.

C. Articles (Refereed Journals)

"Contemporary Afrikaans Fiction in the World: The Englishing of Marlene van Niekerk." *Journal of Commonwealth Studies*, 49.3 (2014), 395-409.

"Many Tongues / Maleme / Talle Tonge / Iilwimi Ngeelwimi / Amalimi Amanengi." *Oxford Literary Review* 36.1 (2014): 155–56.

"The Case for the English Dolnik; or, How Not to Introduce Prosody." *Poetics Today* 33.1 (Spring 2012): 1–26.

"Context, Idioculture, Invention." *New Literary History* 42 (2011): 681–99.

"Afterword: Responsible Reading and Cultural Difference." *Reading after Empire. New Formations* 73 (2011): 117–25. Reprinted in *Postcolonial Audiences: Readers, Viewers and Reception.* Ed. Bethan Benwell, James Procter, and Gemma Robinson. New York: Routledge, 2012. 234–43.

"Once More with Feeling: Fiction, Performance and Affect." *Affects, Text, and Performativity.* Ed. Alex Houen. Special Issue of *Textual Practice* 25.2 (2011): 329–43.

"In Defence of the Dolnik: Twentieth-Century British Verse in Free Four-Beat Metre." *Etudes britanniques contemporaines* 39 (December 2010): 5–18.

"Joyce's Noises." *Sound Effects.* Ed. Chris Jones and Neil Rhodes. Special issue of *Oral Tradition* 24.2 (2009):471–84.

"'News That Stays News': Literature, Invention and Cultural History." *Edda* 109 (2009): 3–8.

"Reading for the Obvious in Poetry: A Conversation between Derek Attridge and Henry Staten" (with Henry Staten). *World Picture* 2 (2008): n. pag. <http://www.worldpicturejournal.com/>.

"Performing Metaphors: The Singularity of Literary Figuration." *The Idea of the Literary.* Ed. Nicholas Harrison. Special issue of *Paragraph* 28.2 (July 2005): 18–34. Polish translation printed in *Tekstualia* 4.31 (2012): 183–97.

"Zoë Wicomb's Home Truths: Place, Genealogy, and Identity in *David's Story*." *Journal of Postcolonial Writing* 41.2 (2005): 156–65.

"Ethical Modernism: Servants as Others in J. M. Coetzee's Early Fiction." *Ethics and Literature.* Ed. Michael Eskin. Special issue of *Poetics Today* 25.4 (Winter 2004): 653–71.

"Nothing to Declare: J. Hillis Miller and Zero's Paradox." *Zero and Literature.* Ed. Rolland Munro. Special issue of *Journal for Cultural Research* 8.2 (April 2004): 115–21.

"Age of Bronze, State of Grace: Music and Dogs in Coetzee's *Disgrace.*" *Novel: A Forum on Fiction* 34.1 (2000): 98–118.

"Judging Joyce." *Modernism/Modernity* 6.3 (1999): 15–32.

"Innovation, Literature, Ethics: Relating to the Other." *PMLA* 114 (1999): 20–31. Reprinted in *Deconstruction: Critical Concepts in Literary and Cultural Studies.* Ed. Jonathan Culler. Vol. 4. London: Routledge, 2003. 325–42.

"A Note on Richard Cureton's Response." *Metrics Today II.* Ed. Christoph Küper. Special issue of *Poetics Today* 17 (1996): 51–54.

"The Postmodernity of Joyce: Chance, Coincidence, and the Reader." *Joyce Studies Annual* 1995 (1995): 10–18.

"Trusting the Other: Ethics and Politics in J. M. Coetzee's *Age of Iron.*" *The Writings of J. M. Coetzee.* Ed. Michael Valdez Moses. Special issue of *South Atlantic Quarterly* 93 (1994): 59–82.

"Arche-Jargon." *Qui Parle* 5.1 (1991). 41–52.

"Rhythm in English Poetry." *New Literary History* 21 (1990): 1015–37. Extract reprinted in *Modern British Literature.* Ed. Laurie Di Mauro. 2nd ed. Farmington Hills: St. James Press, 1999.

"Molly's Flow: The Writing of 'Penelope' and the Question of Women's Language." *Feminist Readings of Joyce.* Ed. Ellen Carol Jones. Special issue of *Modern Fiction Studies* 35 (1989): 543–65.

"Finnegans Awake: The Dream of Interpretation." *James Joyce Quarterly* 27 (1989): 11–29.

"The Backbone of *Finnegans Wake*: Narrative, Digression, and Deconstruction." *Genre* 17 (1984): 375–400. Reprinted in *British Modernist Fiction, 1920 to 1945.* Ed. Harold Bloom. New York: Chelsea House, 1986. 98–108.

"Language as Imitation: Jakobson, Joyce, and the Art of Onomatopoeia." *MLN* 99 (1984): 1116–40.

"The Language of Poetry: Materiality and Meaning." *Essays in Criticism* 31 (1981): 228–45.

"Dryden's Dilemma, or, Racine Refashioned: The Problem of the English Dramatic Couplet." *Yearbook of English Studies* 9 (1979): 55–77.

D. Articles (Nonrefereed Journals and Publications)

"The Humanities without Condition: Derrida and the Singular *Oeuvre.*" *Arts and Humanities in Higher Education* 13.1–2 (2014): 54–61.

"The Sonnet Refashioned: Muldoon's *Maggot.*" *A Between Almanach for the Year 2013.* Ed. Tomasz Wiśniewski. Gdańsk: Maski, 2013. 137–38.

"Introduction to J. M. Coetzee." *A Between Almanach for the Year 2013.* Ed. Tomasz Wiśniewski. Gdańsk: Maski, 2013. 25–26.

"Dobrowolna nieprzejrzystosc. O dzialaniu i zxabieraniu glosu: Z Derekiem Attridge'em rozmawiaja Pawel Moscicki." Interview with Pawel Moscicki. *Wyostrzyć Wzrok. J. M. Coetzee: Sztuka, Świat I Polityka.* Ed. Anna R. Burzyńska and Waldemar Rapior. Krakow: Fundacja Malta, 2012. 19–32.

"Rhythm," "Beat," and "Classical Verse in Modern Languages." *Princeton Encyclopedia of Poetry and Poetics.* Ed. Roland Greene and Stephen Cushman. 4th ed. Princeton: Princeton University Press, 2012.

"'To Speak of This You Would Need the Tongue of a God': Coetzee's *Age of Iron,* Township Violence, and the Classics." *Forum for World Literature Studies* 2.3 (2010): 355–62.

"The Singular Events of Literature." Response to Peter Lamarque. *The British Journal of Aesthetics* 50 (2010): 81–84.

"Derek Attridge on the Ethical Debates in Literary Studies." *Ethics and the Inventive Work.* Ed. Zahi Zalloua. Special issue of *SubStance* 38.3 (2009): 18–30.

"Can We Do Justice to Literature?" *PN Review* 34 (2008): 14–20.

"We've Lost Those Magic Moments." *Times Higher Education* 1 May 2008: 36–39.

"Even the Syllables Delight." *Times Higher Education Supplement* 2 Feb. 2007: 20–21.

"La Herencia de Beckett." *Minerva* 4 (2007): 26–32.

"Putting Practice into the Theory" (with Jane Elliott). *Times Higher Education Supplement* 5 Jan. 2007: 16.

Introduction. *Inner Workings: Literary Essays 2000–2005.* By J. M. Coetzee. London: Harvill Secker, 2007. ix–xiv. French translation, Paris: Editions du Seuil, 2012. Portuguese translation, Brazil: Companhia das Letras, 2012.

"Conjurers Turn Tricks on Wizards' Coat-Tails." Extract from inaugural lecture. *Times Higher Education Supplement* 23 June 2006: 18–19.

"J. M. Coetzee." *Encyclopedia of British Literature.* Ed. David Scott Kastan. Vol. 3. Oxford: Oxford University Press, 2006. 160–69.

"James Joyce" *Encyclopedia of British Literature.* Ed. David Scott Kastan. Vol. 2. Oxford: Oxford University Press, 2006. 33–36.

"J. M. Coetzee." *New Makers of Modern Culture.* Ed. Justin Wintle. Vol. 1. London: Routledge, 2006.

"Finnegans Wake" and "Disgrace." *1001 Books You Must Read before You Die.* Ed. Peter Boxall. London: Quintet Books, 2006.

"A Response to Rob Pope." *Language and Literature* 14 (2005): 390–92.

"Deconstruction Today." *Etudes Anglaises* 1.58 (2005): 42–52.

"Man with a Mission Impossible." *Times Higher Education Supplement* 12 Nov. 2004: xx–xx.

"Jacques Derrida" (with Thomas Baldwin). Obituary. *The Guardian* 11 Oct. 2004: xx–xx.

"Literature, Ethics, Responsibility, Invention, and the Other." *Recherches Anglaises et Nord Américaines* 36 (2003): 35–37.

"Ethics, Otherness, and Literary Form." *European English Messenger* 12.1 (Spring 2003): 33–38.

"Maxima and Beats: A Response to Nigel Fabb's Reply." *Language and Literature* 12.1 (2003): 81–82.

"The Rules of English Metre: A Response to Nigel Fabb." *Language and Literature* 12.1 (2003): 71–72.

"From *Finnegans Wake* to *The Skriker*: Morphing Language in James Joyce and Caryl Churchill." *Papers on Joyce* 7/8 (2001–2002): 45–53.

"J. M. Coetzee's *Boyhood*, Confession, and Truth." *South African Writing at the Crossroads*. Ed. Nahem Yousaf and Graham Pechey. Special issue of *Critical Survey* 11.2 (1999): 77–93.

"The Anxiety of Influence." Editorial board symposium. *Language and Literature* 7 (1998): 78–79.

Literary Form and the Question of Ethics. Pietermaritzburg: University of Natal, 1997. Occasional Papers in English Studies No. 2.

Foreword. *Joyce, Race, and Empire*. By Vincent Cheng. Cambridge: Cambridge University Press, 1995. xi–xiii.

"The Movement of Meaning: Phrasing and Repetition in English Poetry." *Repetition*. Ed. Andreas Fischer. Tübingen: Gunter Narr Verlag, 1994. 61–83. Swiss Papers in English Language and Literature 7.

"Classical Meters in Modern Languages." *The New Princeton Encyclopedia of Poetry and Poetics*. Ed. Alex Preminger and Terence V. Brogan. Princeton: Princeton University Press, 1993.

"Joyce's 'Clay' and the Problem of the Referent." *Le dit et le non-dit*. Ed. Jean-Jacques Lecercle. Special issue of *Tropismes* 6 (1993): 113–30.

"Spenser's Quantitative Verse." *The Spenser Encyclopaedia*. Ed. A. C. Hamilton et al. Toronto: University of Toronto Press, 1990.

"Poetry." *The International Encyclopedia of Communications*. Ed. Erik Barnouw. New York: Annenberg School of Communications and Oxford University Press, 1989.

"Poetry Unbound? Observations on Free Verse." The 1987 Warton Lecture on Poetry. *Proceedings of the British Academy, 1987*. Vol. 73. London: The British Academy, 1989. 353–73.

"Joyce, Jameson, and the Text of History." *Scribble 1: genèse des textes*. Ed. Claude Jacquet. Paris: Minard, 1988. 185–93. La Revue des Lettres Modernes, Série James Joyce 1.

"'Damn with Faint Praise': Double Offbeat Demotion." *Eidos* 4 (1987): 3–6.

E. Book Reviews

The Novel After Theory, by Judith Ryan (Columbia University Press, 2012). *Modern Language Quarterly*, forthcoming.

A Passion for Joyce: The Letters of Hugh Kenner and Adaline Glasheen, ed. Edward M. Burns (UCD Press, 2008). *James Joyce Broadsheet* 89 (June 2011): 1.

Who's Afraid of James Joyce? by Karen Lawrence (University Press of Florida, 2010). *Modernism/Modernity* 18.2 (2011): 482–84.

In Memory of Jacques Derrida, by Nicholas Royle (Edinburgh University Press, 2009). *Oxford Literary Review* 33.1 (2011): 131–33.

Encountering "Disgrace": Reading and Teaching Coetzee's Novel, by Bill McDonald (Camden House, 2009). *English* 228.60 (2011): 94–96.

Ambiguities of Witnessing: Law and Literature in the Time of a Truth Commission, by Mark Sanders (Stanford University Press, 2007). *Journal of Postcolonial Writing* 45.2 (Summer 2009): 235–36.

Nile Baby, by Elleke Boehmer (Ayebia Clarke Publishing, 2008). *Postcolonial Studies Association Newsletter* May 2009: 10–11.

Radical Atheism: Derrida and the Time of Life, by Martin Hägglund (Stanford University Press, 2008). *Derrida Today* 2.2 (2009): 271–81.

Imagining Joyce and Derrida: Between "Finnegans Wake" and "Glas," by Peter Mahon (University of Toronto Press, 2007). *James Joyce Literary Supplement* 22.2 (Fall 2008): 10–11.

"A Portrait of the Artist as a Young Man" by James Joyce, ed. John Paul Riquelme (Norton, 2007). *James Joyce Broadsheet* 80 (June 2008): 2.

Rewriting Modernity: Studies in Black South African Literary History, by David Attwell (Ohio University Press, 2006). *Research in African Literatures* 39 (2008): 150–51.

"A Return to Form?" *Reading for Form* (University of Washington Press, 2006), by Susan J. Wolfson and Marshall Brown; *How to Read a Poem*

(Blackwell, 2007), by Terry Eagleton; *On Form: Poetry, Aestheticism, and the Legacy of a Word* (Oxford University Press, 2007), by Angela Leighton; *Our Secret Discipline: Yeats and Lyric Form* (Oxford University Press, 2007), by Helen Vendler; and *The Secret Life of Poems: A Poetry Primer* (Faber and Faber, 2008), by Tom Paulin. *Textual Practice* 22.3 (2008): 563–75. Polish translation printed in *Poeci współcześni. Poeci przeszłości*. Ed. Monika Szuby and Tomasza Wiśniewskiego. Gdańsk: Uniwersytet Gdański, 2013. 19–42.

The Philosophy of Derrida, by Mark Dooley and Liam Kavanagh (Acumen, 2007). *Times Higher Education Supplement* 6 Apr. 2007: 26–27.

The Flowers of Tarbes or, Terror in Literature, by Jean Paulhan. Trans. and introduction by Michael Syrotinski (University of Illinois Press, 2006). *Cambridge Quarterly* 36.2 (2007): 175–77.

Writing in Crisis: Ethics and History in Gordimer, Ndebele and Coetzee, by Stefan Helgesson (University of KwaZulu-Natal Press, 2004). *Research in African Literatures* 36.3 (Fall 2005): 154–55.

Suspicious Readings of Joyce's Dubliners, by Margot Norris (University of Pennsylvania Press, 2003). *James Joyce Quarterly* 41 (2004): 541–44.

The Origins of Criticism: Literary Culture and Poetic Theory in Classical Greece, by Andrew Ford (Princeton, 2002). *The Cambridge Quarterly* 33.1 (2004): 51–54.

James Joyce: The Finnegans Wake *Notebooks*, ed. Vincent Deane, Daniel Ferrer, and Geert Lernout (Brepols, 2001–2002). *Modernism/Modernity* 10.3 (September 2003): 571–73.

Finnegans Wake, by James Joyce, ed. and dir. Roger Marsh (Naxos Audiobooks, 1998). *James Joyce Literary Supplement* 13.2 (Fall 1999): 8–9.

Joyce's Abandoned Female Costumes, Gratefully Received, by Elisabeth Sheffield (Fairleigh Dickinson University Press, 1998). *James Joyce Broadsheet* 52 (February, 1999): 2.

Joyce, Chaos, and Complexity, by Thomas Jackson Rice (University of Illinois Press, 1997). *South Atlantic Review* 62 (1997): 104–06.

Citation and Modernity: Derrida, Joyce, and Brecht, by Claudette Sartiliot (University of Oklahoma Press, 1993). *James Joyce Quarterly* 34 (1996–1997): 183–87.

The Fictions of James Joyce and Wyndham Lewis: Monsters of Nature and Design, by Scott Klein (Cambridge University Press, 1994). *Modern Philology* 94 (1997): 549–52.

"Beyond Metrics." *Rhythmic Phrasing in English Verse* (Longman, 1992), by Richard Cureton. *Metrics Today II.* Ed. Christoph Küper. Special issue of *Poetics Today* 17 (1996): 9–27.

James Joyce and the Language of History, Robert Spoo (Oxford University Press, 1994). *Modern Fiction Studies* 42 (1996): 888–90.

Finnegans Wake, by James Joyce, read by Patrick Healy (Rennicks Auriton Publishing, 1992). *James Joyce Quarterly* 32 (1994): 130–32.

A Story of South Africa: J. M. Coetzee's Fiction in Context, by Susan VanZanten Gallagher (Harvard University Press, 1991). *Novel: A Forum on Fiction* 26 (1993): 321–23.

Jocoserious Joyce: The Fate of Folly in Ulysses, by Robert H. Bell (Cornell University Press, 1991); *Narrative Con/Texts in* Ulysses, by Bernard Benstock (University of Illinois Press, 1991); and *Wandering and Return in Finnegans Wake*, by Kimberly J. Devlin (Princeton University Press, 1991). *Modern Fiction Studies* 38 (1992), 514–17.

Joyce and the Law of the Father, by Frances L. Restuccia (Yale University Press, 1989); and *Writing Joyce: A Semiotics of the Joyce System*, by Lorraine Weir (Indiana University Press, 1989). *Yearbook of English Studies* 22 (1992): 344–45.

The Novel as Family Romance: Language, Gender, and Authority from Fielding to Joyce, by Christine van Boheemen (Cornell University Press, 1987). *James Joyce Literary Supplement* 2.2 (1988): 7–8.

Myriad-Minded Man: Jottings on Joyce, ed. Rosa-Maria Bosinelli, Paola Pugliatti, and Romana Zacchi (CLUEB, 1986). *James Joyce Literary Supplement* 1.2 (1987): 12.

How Poetry Works, by Philip Davies Roberts (Viking-Penguin, 1986). *Style* 21 (1987): 143–47.

Rewriting the Renaissance: The Discourses of Sexual Difference in Early Modern Europe, ed. Margaret W. Ferguson, Maureen Quilligan, and Nancy J. Vickers (University of Chicago Press, 1986). *Renaissance Quarterly* 40 (1987): 810–14.

Joyce's Dislocations: Essays on Reading as Translation, by Fritz Senn (Johns Hopkins University Press, 1984). *James Joyce Broadsheet* 19 (February 1986): 1.

Ulysses: The Corrected Text, by James Joyce, ed. Hans Walter Gabler (Penguin, 1986). *James Joyce Broadsheet* 21 (October 1986): 2.

Structuralism, by John Sturrock (Paladin, 1986). *Times Literary Supplement* 21 Nov. 1986: 1306.

Vision and Resonance: Two Senses of Poetic Form, by John Hollander, 2nd
ed. (Oxford University Press, 1985). *Times Literary Supplement* 28 Mar.
1986: 343.

The Living Lyre in English Verse from Elizabeth through the Restoration,
by Louise Schleiner (University of Missouri Press, 1984). *Renaissance
Quarterly* 39 (1986): 134–36.

Le Vers de Shakespeare, by Henri Suhamy (Didier, 1984). *Eidos* 2.1–2 (1985): 3.

The Classics and English Renaissance Poetry: Three Case Studies, by Gordon
Braden (Yale University Press, 1978). *Modern Language Review* 76 (1981):
437–38.

*The Peacocks and the Bourgeoisie: Ironic Vision in Patrick White's Shorter
Prose Fiction*, by David Myers (Adelaide University Press, 1978). *Journal
of English and Germanic Philology* 79 (1980): 150–52.

French Poets and the English Renaissance: Studies in Fame and Transformation,
by Ann Lake Prescott (Yale University Press, 1978). *English Language
Notes* 17 (1979): 136–39.

Words into Rhythm: English Speech Rhythm in Verse and Prose, by D. W.
Harding (Cambridge University Press, 1976). *Poetics and Theory of
Literature* 4 (1979): 196–201.

Vision and Resonance: Two Senses of Poetic Form, by John Hollander (Oxford
University Press, 1975). *Modern Language Review* 72 (1977): 649–51.

English Prosody from Chaucer to Wyatt, by Jack Connor (Mouton, 1974).
Modern Language Review 72 (1977): 147–48.

II. AS EDITOR

A. Books

The Cambridge History of South African Literature (coedited with David
Attwell; coauthored introduction, 1–13, and headnotes). Cambridge:
Cambridge University Press, 2012.

Theory after "Theory" (coedited with Jane Elliott; coauthored "Theory's
Nine Lives," introduction, 1–15). London: Routledge, 2011 (cloth and
paperback). Arabic translation forthcoming.

James Joyce's Ulysses: *A Casebook* (with Introduction, 3–16, and suggested
readings). Oxford: Oxford University Press, 2004 (cloth and paperback).
Introduction reprinted in booklet accompanying *Ulysses*. Dir. Roger
Marsh. Naxos AudioBooks, 2004.

Semicolonial Joyce (coedited with Marjorie Howes; coauthored introduction, 1–20). Cambridge: Cambridge University Press, 2000 (cloth and paperback).

Writing South Africa: Literature, Apartheid, and Democracy 1970–1995 (coedited with Rosemary Jolly; coauthored introduction, 1–13, and selected bibliography). Cambridge: Cambridge University Press, 1998 (cloth and paperback).

Acts of Literature. By Jacques Derrida (authored "Derrida and the Questioning of Literature," introduction, 1–19; "This Strange Institution Called Literature," interview, 33–75; headnotes; and selected bibliography). London: Routledge, 1992 (cloth and paperback). Korean translation, South Korea: Moonji Publishing, 2012. Interview reprinted in Polish translation in *Literatura na świeci* 11–12 (1999): 176–225. Introduction and interview reprinted in Czech translation in *Aluze* 2 (2000): 102–50. Interview reprinted in the original French in *Derrida d'ici, Derrida de là.* Ed. Thomas Dutoit. Paris: Galilée, 2009. 253–92. Interview reprinted in Lithuanian translation in *Baltos Lankos* 33 (2010): 86–128.

The Cambridge Companion to James Joyce (authored chronology and further reading). Cambridge: Cambridge University Press, 1990 (cloth and paperback). Reprint edition, Shanghai: Shanghai Foreign Language Education Press, 2000. Revised edition with new essays, 2004.

The Linguistics of Writing: Arguments between Language and Literature (coedited with Nigel Fabb, Alan Durant, and Colin MacCabe). Manchester: Manchester University Press, 1987; New York: Routledge, 1988 (cloth and paperback). Translated into Spanish as *La Lingüística de la escritura: Debates entre lengua y literatura.* Trans. Javier Yagüe Bosch. Madrid: Visor, 1989.

Post-Structuralism and the Question of History (coedited with Geoff Bennington and Robert Young). Cambridge: Cambridge University Press, 1987. Paperback edition, 1989. Chinese translation, Beijing: Beijing Normal University Press, 2006.

Post-Structuralist Joyce: Essays from the French (coedited with Daniel Ferrer; coauthored "Highly Continental Evenements," introduction, 1–13). Cambridge: Cambridge University Press, 1984 (cloth and paperback).

B. Journal Special Issue

J. M. Coetzee's Disgrace (coedited with Peter D. McDonald and authored introduction). Special issue of *Interventions: International Journal of Postcolonial Studies* 4.3 (2002).

III. ELECTRONIC AND BROADCAST MEDIA

"Joyce in Southern Africa: A Response by Derek Atrridge to Ariela Freedman's 'Global Joyce.'" *Literature Compass* 8.11 (November 2011): 870–72.

"'To Speak of This You Would Need the Tongue of a God': On Representing the Trauma of Township Violence." *Philia&Filia* 1.2 (2010). <http://seer.ufrgs.br/Philiaefilia>.

"Ethics, Hospitality and Radical Atheism: A Dialogue." Debate with Martin Hägglund. iTunes University and University of Oxford, 2010. Podcast.

"'News That Stays News': Literature and Historical Distance." *Moveable Type* 4 (2008). <http://www.ucl.ac.uk/english/graduate/issue/4/currentissue.html>.

Interview with Mark Thwaite. *ReadySteadyBook.* ReadySteadyBook, 2005. <http://www.readysteadybook.com/Article.aspx?page=derekattridge>.

"Following Derrida." *Khoraographies: Ad Honorem Jacques Derrida.* Ed. Dragan Kujundzic. Special issue of *Tympanum* 4 (2000). <www.usc.edu/dept/comp-lit/tympanum/4/khora.html>.

"Linguistics and Poetics Revisited: Response." *Versification.* n.p., 1998. <http://www.arsversificandi.net/resources/ papers/mla97/attridge.html>.

Interview with David Erben, Christopher Tidwell, and Walt Lewallen. *Seulemonde* 4 (1997). <http://nosferatu.cas.usf/journal/>.

"Remembering Berni Benstock." *Hypermedia Joyce Studies* 1.1 (1995). <http://hjs.ff.cuni.cz/archives/v1/hjs.html>.

Rhythm in English Poetry. Australian Broadcasting Corporation. 1989. Radio.